Soloing Techniques for Beginners

11 Guitar Techniques Every Rock and Blues Guitarist Must Know With 125+ Licks You Can Play Today

GUITAR HEAD

GH@theguitarhead.com
www.facebook.com/theguitarhead/

©Copyright 2021 by Guitar Head — All rights reserved.

This document is geared towards providing exact and reliable information in regards to the topic and issue covered. The publication is sold with the idea that the publisher is not required to render accounting, officially permitted, or otherwise, qualified services. If advice is necessary, legal or professional, a practiced individual in the profession should be ordered.

From a Declaration of Principles which was accepted and approved equally by a Committee of the American Bar Association and a Committee of Publishers and Associations.

In no way is it legal to reproduce, duplicate, or transmit any part of this document in either electronic means or in printed format. Recording of this publication is strictly prohibited and any storage of this document is not allowed unless with written permission from the publisher. All rights reserved.

The information provided herein is stated to be truthful and consistent, in that any liability, in terms of inattention or otherwise, by any usage or abuse of any policies, processes, or directions contained within is the solitary and utter responsibility of the recipient reader. Under no circumstances will any legal responsibility or blame be held against the publisher for any reparation, damages, or monetary loss due to the information herein, either directly or indirectly.

Respective authors own all copyrights not held by the publisher.

The information herein is offered for informational purposes solely, and is universal as so. The presentation of the information is without contract or any type of guarantee assurance.

The trademarks that are used are without any consent, and the publication of the trademark is without permission or backing by the trademark owner. All trademarks and brands within this book are for clarifying purposes only and are the owned by the owners themselves, not affiliated with this document.

Disclaimer

Please note the information contained within this document is for educational and entertainment purposes only. Every attempt has been made to provide accurate, up to date and reliable complete information. No warranties of any kind are expressed or implied. Readers acknowledge that the author is not engaging in the rendering of legal and financial, medical or professional advice. The content of this book has been derived from various sources. Please consult a licensed professional before attempting any techniques outlined in this book.

By reading this document, the reader agrees that under no circumstances are is the author responsible for any losses, direct or indirect, which are incurred as a result of the use of the information contained within this document, including, but not limited to, — errors, omissions, or inaccuracies.

Table of Contents

Free Audio Tracks and Bonuses **5**

Introduction. **8**

Chapter 1: Alternate Picking **11**
   All About Alternate Picking. 12

Chapter 2: Palm Muting Technique **29**
   Learning The Technique. 30

Chapter 3: Vibrato. **43**
   Vibrating The Daylight Out of the Note. 45

Chapter 4: Legato **56**
   Hammers and Pulls 57

Chapter 5: Bending **66**
   Bending the String Right 67
   Licks Worth Knowing 73

Chapter 6: Economy Picking — You May Know It as Sweep Picking . . **81**
   The Technique 82

Chapter 7: Hybrid Picking — Using Pick and Fingers **91**
   The Era of Hybrid 92

Chapter 8: Tapping **99**
   Tap Your Notes Away 99

Chapter 9: Harmonics **108**
   Purity of Harmonics 108

Chapter 10: Whammy Bar 113
    Understanding the Whammy Bar 113

Chapter 11: Octave Playing 121
    Getting the Basics 121

Farewell! 127

Free Audio Tracks and Bonuses

Congratulations on selecting a Guitar Head book. If it's your first time getting one of our books, I want to welcome you to our little world.

At Guitar Head, our mission is *to help you find a purpose with guitar so you can find happiness and identity in it.*

This mission comes from the special bond I share with my guitar. My guitar has been by my side since I was 12. I started playing as a way to look cool in school but it soon grew to be something much bigger than that. It gave me something to work on every day, it gave me excitement in life, it gave me access to some very talented people and the best thing of all — it gave me an identity which I wear proudly — the identity of a guitarist!

And now, with Guitar Head — I want to help you create the same relationship with the guitar.

I've seen far too many guitarists — pros and beginners alike — failing to create a connection with the guitar. They concentrate only on the mechanics of playing guitar — playing faster, playing more songs, playing techniques, getting your fingers to do that, do this……… without really taking the time to build a relationship with the instrument.

With Guitar Head, I want to change things around! I want to help you build a relationship with the guitar. I want to make guitar your partner through the ups and downs of life — not just a musical instrument that you can play. Something that can give you happiness and energy, something that can be your escape during dark times, something that will give you access to talented people, something that can give you all the confidence in the world.

And how do you do that? — You build a relationship with your guitar. You find a strong purpose with music and guitar! That's what Guitar Head is all about. That's what we do and that's what we want to help you do.

Now, I'll need more than half a page to help you find your purpose and relationship with the guitar. Hence, let's continue this discussion through email. This section was intended only to give you a brief introduction of what we stand for and how we can help you on your guitar journey.

Download any of the bonuses below to become an email subscriber and we can continue our conversation there. I'll see you in your inbox!

Oh, one more thing! You can also get the below bonuses for free when you sign up to be a part of Guitar Head. They're tools that'll help your guitar journey and help you use this book the way it was intended to be used. Go get your hands on it before you start the book — you don't want to stop the book midway, download the bonuses and come back.

Here is a list of bonuses that you get with this book:

1. **Audio Tracks:** The audio tracks provided with this book are an integral part of the content. It ensures that you are playing the charts and chords the way it was intended to be played.

2. **A Free Book:** Guitar mastery is all about nailing those small elements and avoiding mistakes. In this book, I explain 25 such mistakes and provide ways to avoid them.

3. **Access to a private community of passionate guitarists:** Being around like-minded people is the first step in being successful at anything. The Guitar Head community is full of passionate guitarists who help each other excel. When you buy a Guitar Head book, you automatically become a part of this amazing community of people who are willing to listen to your music, answer your questions or talk anything guitar.

4. **Weekly Guitar Lessons:** Every Saturday — you'll receive a fresh piece of content delivered right to your inbox. The lessons range from things like *How to buy your first guitar* to *Tabs to your favorite songs*.

You can follow the below link to become a subscriber and get your hands on all the above bonuses:

www.theguitarhead.com/bonus

P.S. Write to support@theguitarhead.com if you need help downloading the bonuses.

Introduction

Guitar licks sound a lot like guitar riffs, and it is easy to see why people are often confused. I too was under the same impression once, until someone decided to correct me and show me how wrong I was. For those of you who may not know the difference, let me give you a quick introduction about what guitar licks are. Oh, and don't be ashamed if you didn't know. You'd be surprised to learn that there is a vast majority of guitarists who still cannot differentiate between a lick and a riff.

A riff is essentially a thematic part of a song. It is created as the main part of said song. The riff is created using chords or notes, and these are often repeated throughout the song. A riff can have variations, change of keys, however, it is always easy to understand and stands out as a unique element of the song.

When it comes to a lick, things are pretty much the same, with only one major difference. You see, while the riffs are repeated and contain variation, licks are essentially specific parts of any song. Furthermore, it is through using numerous licks that you end up creating a riff. A riff cannot be a lick, but a lick can lead into a riff.

Unlike the riff, a lick is neither the main section of the song, nor complete in nature.

"Well, why on earth are we learning it then?"

Good question. While it is easy to copy someone else's work and riffs, you need to establish a good understanding about licks if you are to take your playing up a notch. These are also vital to provide you with the fillers you need when your soundtrack feels like it is missing something. It is the small detail that matters the most, and it is through these licks that you can finally step in and say "I got that covered."

Licks are transferable, meaning that you can use your favorite variation of licks in other songs without any problem. All you need is to know your scales. As long as that is sorted, there is nothing stopping you from playing some exquisite and delicious licks, stunning the band members and wowing the crowd.

Therefore, *Guitar Techniques Demystified* is going to be your guide to teach you all about licks and how you can use them to take your skills up a level. I will be sharing with you a variety of licks, all reflecting styles adopted by renowned guitarists such as:

- John Petrucci
- Steve Vai
- Greg Howe
- Brian May
- Joe Satriani
- Tim Miller
- Jimi Hendrix
- Eric Clapton

These are just some of the many names you will come across in this book. Of course, there is no point in playing exactly the same notes and licks these great artists have gone on to immortalize. That would be cheating, and frankly, it wouldn't serve us with any purpose. The point is to play like them and create our own unique licks.

All of the licks that you will come across are just to guide you on how licks are formed, played and performed. Once you are comfortable using them, go crazy with your creativity. That is where the true learning lies.

The book will be using both tablature and standard notation representations. This means that you will be coming across a lot of symbols from music theories. Ideally, you would be someone who knows how to read music. However, if you aren't, the tablature form will help you know the shape and the places of every note that will be played in each lick. See? I told you I got you covered!

To make the most of this book, be sure to play along as you learn. The book isn't meant to be read in one swift go. Instead, take your time and develop an understanding of the licks we will be looking at, and try to understand how they are played. Once comfortable, move on to the next one. This way, you would always know what you have learned, and whether you will be able to play it easily or not.

I believe we are all set to get started. With that said, saddle up, plug in your guitar, keep a metronome handy (you will need it), and let's get started.

CHAPTER 1:

Alternate Picking

Alternate picking is one of the most effective ways to speed up your playing. You cannot expect to play sixteenth notes in succession without breaking the rhythm that easily. To help you ease things, you can use the alternate picking style to speed things along. It feels more natural, it is more comfortable, and you are playing twice the note in a single motion.

This isn't exactly a technique of playing that is limited to specific guitar players. The fact is that every guitarist uses alternate picking every now and then. However, if you still wish to get to know some of the most famous players who continue to showcase their sublime skills using alternate picking technique, they are:

- Steve Morse
- John Petrucci
- Yngwie Malmsteen (Yes, it is hard to pronounce)

So then, the most logical thing for us to do first would be to get ourselves familiarized with alternate picking and then move on to do our first few licks and exercises using the alternate picking technique.

All About Alternate Picking

As a beginner, it is only natural that you may find yourself playing every note with a downward stroke. That is perfectly okay, but not for long though. Once you get comfortable with your pick position, and you have a sense of which string the pick will go on to play, it is time to change things and get into the habit of alternate picking. The sooner you learn it, the lesser the challenges you will face in future.

Your pick position matters a lot, meaning that having the pick in the wrong position might cause you to miss out on the string completely, or play the wrong string instead. This happens to the best of us in the start, but once we understand how alternate picking works, things start making sense, and strings start making music.

To get started, grab your pick and hold it between your thumb and index finger (see picture below). You would want to make sure that only a tiny bit of the pointy end sticks out from your fingers. If you can see a lot, it would cause you to get stuck between strings, or even drop your pick when playing.

Another thing to do is to ensure that your pick is not parallel to the strings. It is wise to have your pick at an angle (around 45 degrees) as that ensures your pick glides instead of jamming up between strings.

Keep the tip of your pick close to the string you intend to play. Keep it too far and you might miss out on the beat, or even miss out the string altogether. Keeping it as close as possible allows you to increase the versatility and speed.

Finally, to play the notes, use your wrist to do the movement. It should move sideways, not up and down. This may take some getting used to, which is why it is a good idea to place your wrist on a flat surface, and then pretend you have a pick. Move your wrist left and right in rhythmic patterns.

It does take practice, and for that, here is a terrific exercise to get your started.

In the picture below, we begin from the top string 'E.' That is to say the thickest string on the guitar. We will begin from the fifth fret position. For now, we will stick to the 'E' string. We will begin by playing only four notes, starting from the fifth and ending at the eighth. The special characters indicate the stroke, meaning that 'Dw' represents a downward stroke and the 'Up' represents an upward stroke.

Look at the picture below, set your metronome to bpm 80, and practice playing each note at every tick of the metronome. Once you are comfortable, start playing the pattern but this time play two notes per tick using a down and an up stoke.

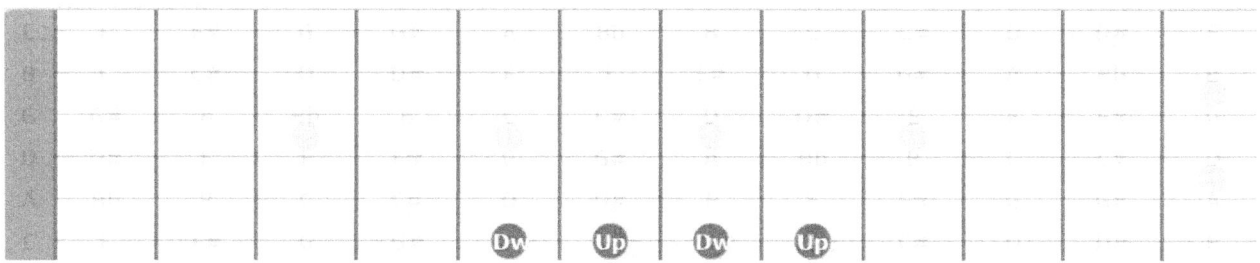

Easy, right? Now let's kick things up a notch. Start as you normally would, by playing these four notes. However, at the end, continue your alternate picking and start going back to the fifth, one fret at a time. See how long you can go back and forth without breaking the rhythm.

Okay, hopefully you were able to do the above with relative ease. It is time for us to make things a little more interesting. Using the same back and forth technique, let us add three more strings to the table.

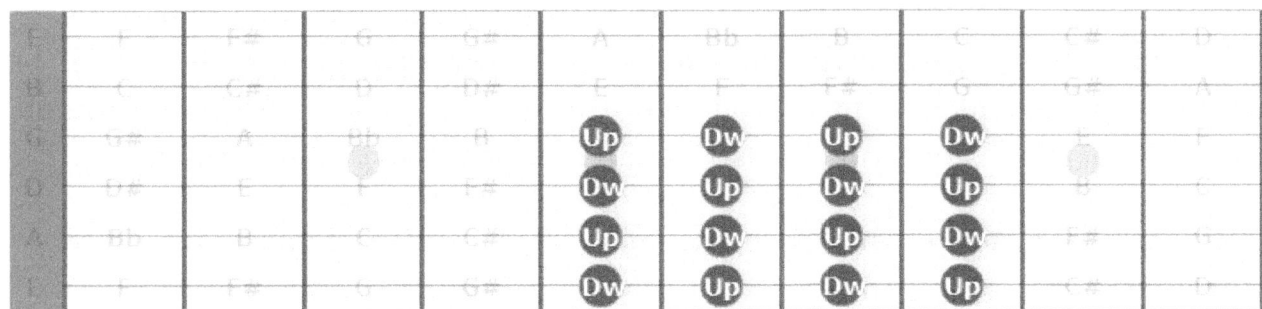

Start from the sixth string, all the way to the last note on the third string (G). Once there, make your way back up. Ensure that you follow the strokes properly as this will help you gain more command on your playing skills.

Done? That wasn't so bad now, was it? Well, that's because we did not use any specific scale or specialized pattern to play these notes. It was more of a warm up exercise to get your fingers and wrist ready for some serious learning.

Before you do move ahead, if you were using just one or two fingers to hold the fret positions, stop right here. By doing so, you will eventually develop a habit of using only one or two fingers, and you will never be able to truly utilize speed, accuracy, or reach, and that will cause you to suffer as a guitarist in the future (emphasize on 'will').

Here is a little diagram to show you how a true guitarist would use his fingers to press the fret positions properly.

Of course — You flip the image if you are using your right hand to hold the fretboard instead!

Next, we will now begin by using the newly acquired skill of alternate picking to play a major and a minor scale. I assure you, it is easier than it looks.

For this exercise, we will be first using the A minor pentatonic scale. While I certainly do hope that most of us are familiar with the key positions, and what exactly a scale is, for those who may not know, the diagram below shows just what I am on about. The beauty is that you can change the root note and it will become a minor scale of the new root you choose. The pattern will remain the same.

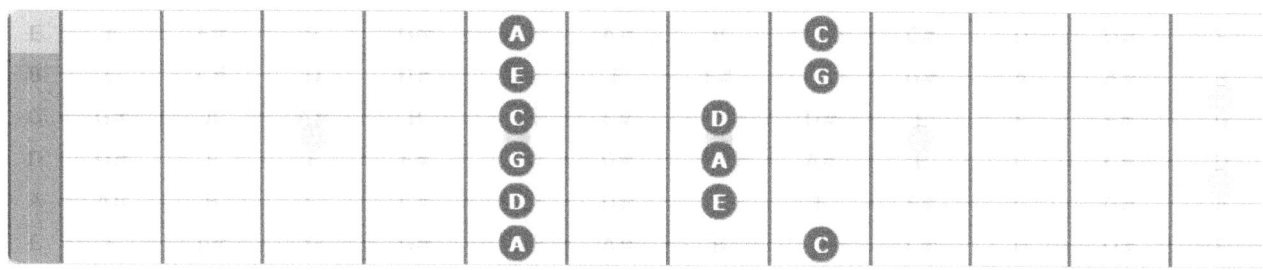

A-Minor Pentatonic

While this may be a scale pattern, the beauty is that you can begin anywhere and end anywhere you like to create your own lick. It is a neat little trick, but works beautifully on songs with an A minor key. You can always refer to the circle of fourths/fifths, which basically show what other keys you can use to create smooth progressions.

Now for the fun part — set the metronome to 90 bpm, and use the alternate picking technique to play the above scale. The goal is to get comfortable and have no irregular switch from notes or strings. If you are able to achieve that, bravo!

Comfortable? Let's change the scale from minor to Major. See if you can spot the difference in the sound.

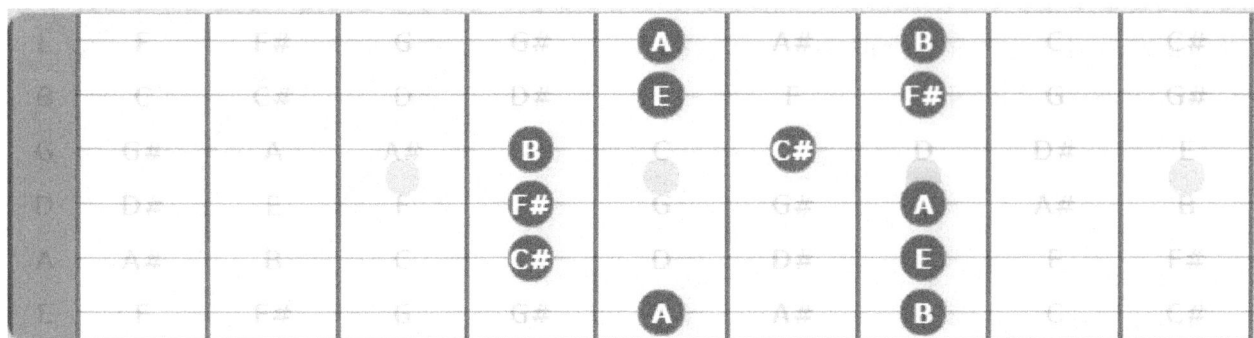

I am sure you were able to figure out how the two sounded a little different. For now, just remember the patterns. There are many patterns and shapes out there that if I was to write a book about scales alone, I would have numerous titles under my name.

Feels too easy? Don't worry. Here is another pattern that I recommend getting used to. This one is a variation of A major as the root note is the first note you will play on the sixth string at fret number five.

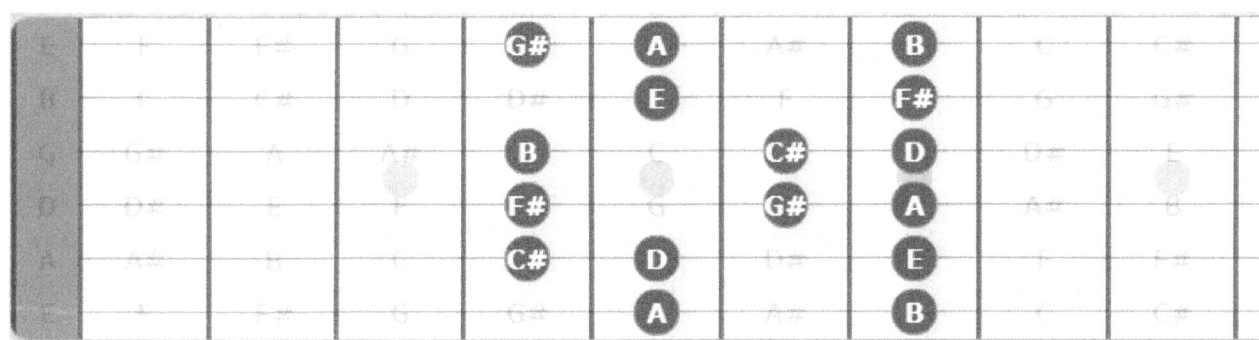

A Major variation

By now, your alternate picking should be gaining some pace. You should be able to coordinate your hand and fret position in a manner that most of your notes play out right. If you cannot play all the notes successfully, without breaking the flow and tempo, or without missing, I suggest you practice first before moving on. The point isn't about how quickly you can learn, but how much of it you can actually apply.

Before we dive into some really, really tougher ones, let me give you one brilliant exercise that will help you for years to come. It is a blend of ascending and descending order. For this exercise, I have chosen the above A major variation pattern, but have started from the eighth fret. Set the tempo low and gradually build up speed once you start hitting the notes right without missing any out.

We will also be leaving the above representation, just for a bit, so that I can bring your attention to the kind of presentation professionals use. It will contain both the standard notations and the tabs. It is probably a good idea to get used to this as you will be seeing a lot of these in this book and throughout your musical career.

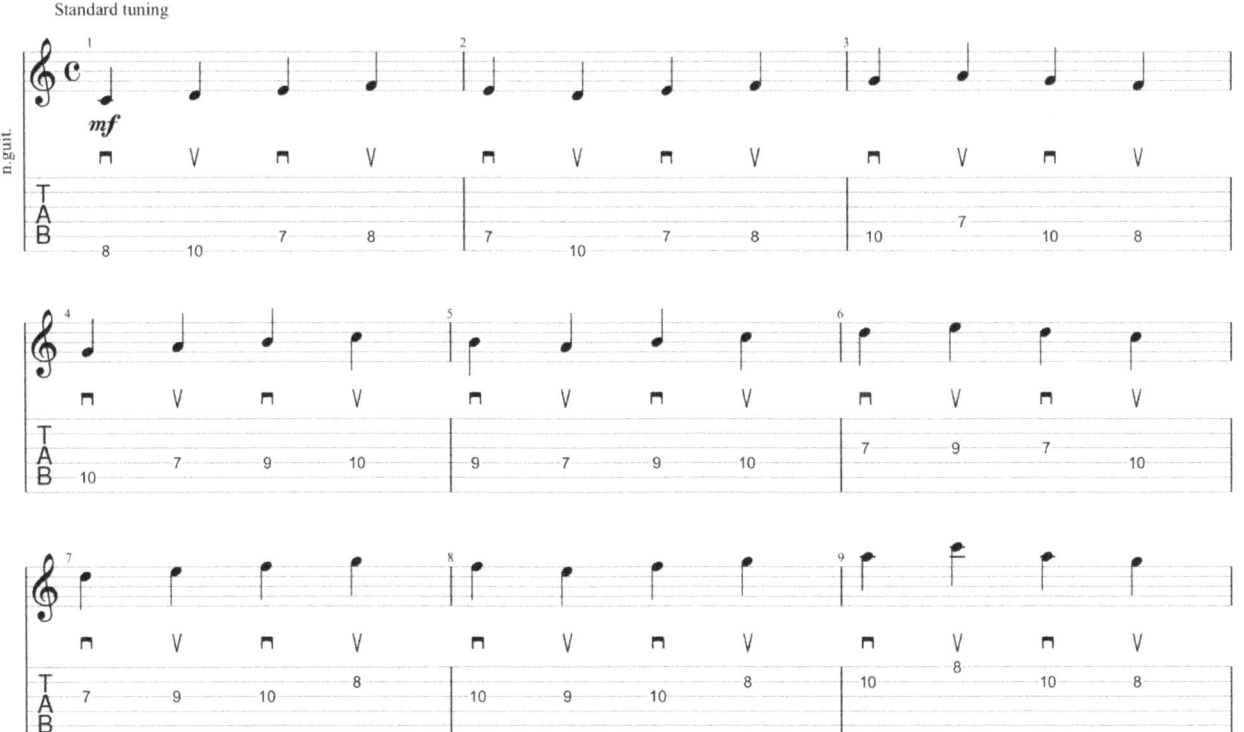

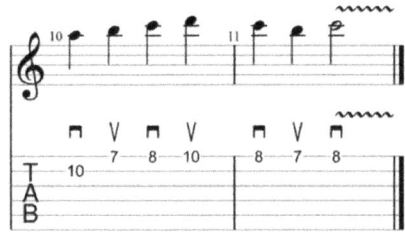

Do not be alarmed with the above representation. Let me quickly give you a tour of what's going on here.

The first line shows the standard notation using the notoriously famous 'treble clef' sign. Following that are the notes. In this instance, we are using the quarter notes (the ones we play once every click of the metronome. In the end, you would notice some wavy lines. Those represent a vibrato using the left hand (the one that holds the neck/frets). Finally, the line that follows underneath the treble clef is the tablature form. That one is pretty obvious. It shows six lines, and we have six strings.

If you cannot read music, you can use these to follow along. The little symbols right above the tab line shows which stroke you need (down or up). The rectangular one means down while the 'V' shaped one means up. Now that you know, take your time to play these notes.

The above is a variation of what we call an Ionian scale. In the simplest words, it is one that moves the standard notation one level above/below, hence changing the notes and playing literally everything in that scale. Here is a representation of how a standard Ionian scale would look like.

Let's continue with another exercise. This time, we will be using the eighth notes, followed by sixteenth notes, and we will be following a descending pattern.

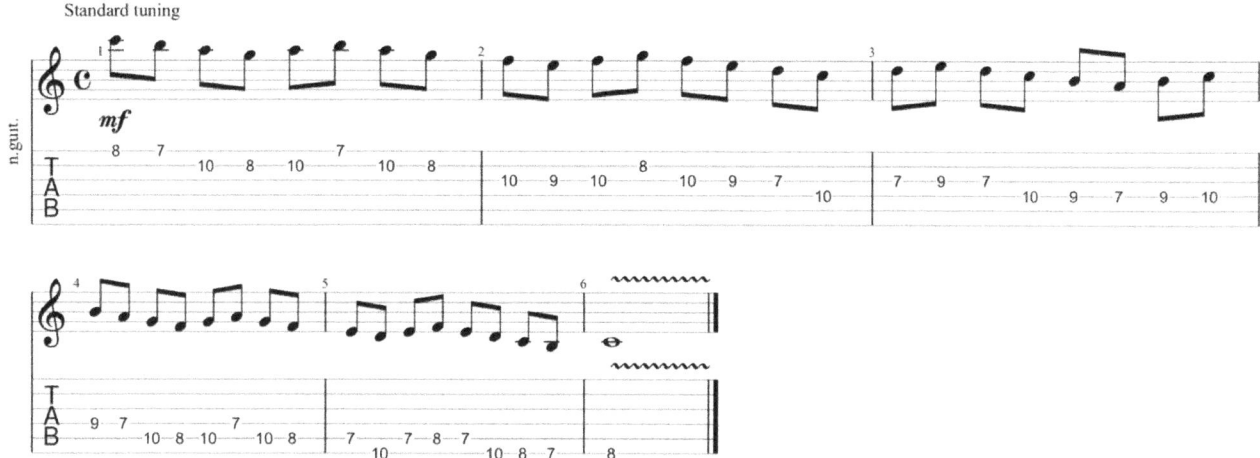

This will need some practice. The focus is not speed, it is the accuracy and smoothness that you should be aiming for. Trust me, speed never impresses the audience as much as clarity and the execution of notes. Get that right and speed will come to you naturally.

Now, let us try the same but instead of using eighth notes, we will use sixteenth notes instead. This exercise will eventually start building up your speed and understanding of how speed goes on to create challenges to keep pace with the tempo. Even the slowest tempos would seem significantly faster when you try to play more notes within the same duration.

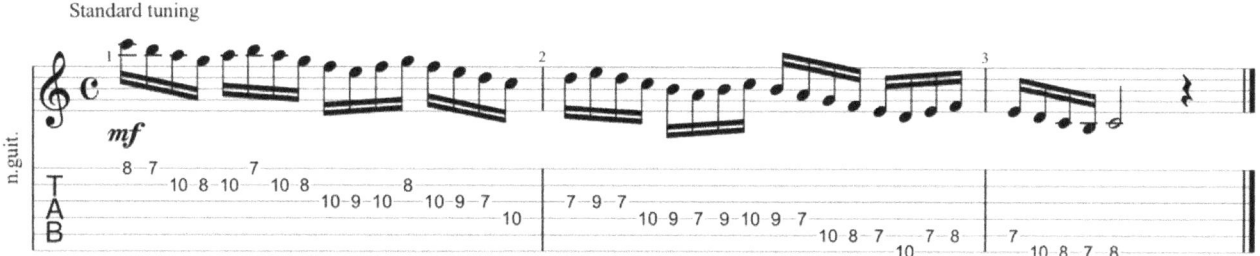

That was fast, even at a tempo as slow as 80 bpm, wasn't it? It takes time, and it takes a lot of practice before you are able to do this one, let alone do licks. However, keep the practice going, and keep using alternate picking. One final exercise before we start with the serious stuff. This one is designed to get you comfortable with solos and licks which may demand you to skip a string or two to continue playing. Begin the below exercise with an upstroke so that every time you change string, you will always be picking in the natural flow. The following uses a .

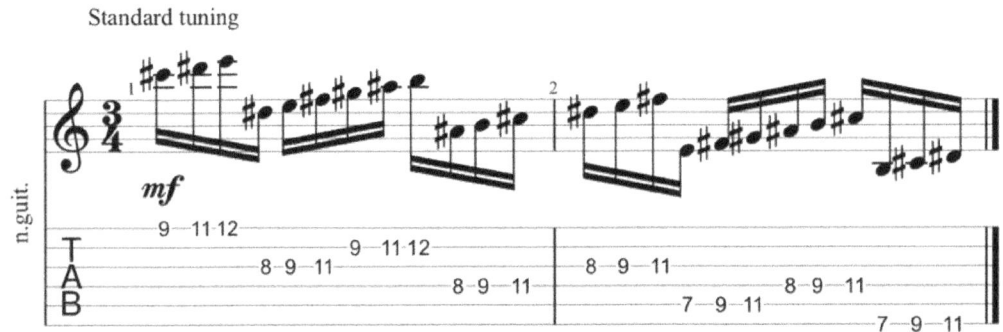

Okay, I admit the sixteenth note would sound insanely difficult. If that isn't your cup of tea at the moment, switch to a slower version. Once again, speed isn't our goal; it is the execution.

So far so good. Time now to learn a Major scale in thirds (two octaves). Sounds a little technical, but once again it is nothing to fear.

Technically speaking, every scale has a third, provided you emphasize it. To make things a little more easier to understand, here is a great method to find out the thirds of any given major scale. Play the first note, skip, and play the third not. The third note is that special note I was referring to. It is often referred to as the "broken third."

Let's take C major scale as an example. If you wish to play the C major scale in thirds, you will need to play the following pattern.

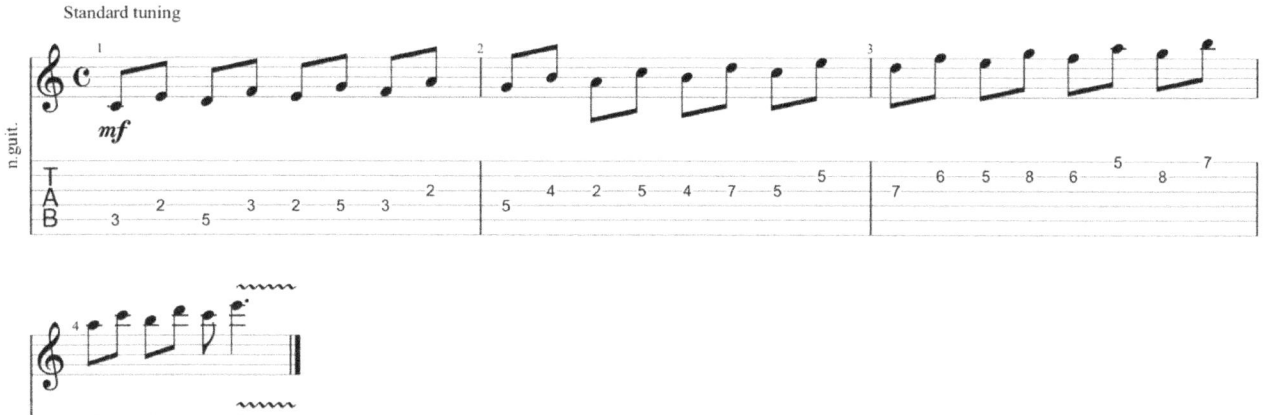

Have a look at the positions. If we pay close attention to the first section, it starts from the root note of C on the fifth string. We play the root note, meaning the first note, skip the second note, which would have been on the fifth fret of the same string, and instead play the next one on the next string. The entire arrangement above follows the same principle — Play first, skip the second and play the third.

Here's a quick challenge. You made your way with the ascending order. Now try and descend using the same technique. Oh, and here's a hint: It's exactly the same.

Don't worry if you weren't able to figure it out. Just play all the notes starting from the last and ending at the first, in that order. Your alternate picking should help you further ease the switch from one string to the other.

Remember I told you that this is called the "broken thirds?" The reason is simple; we are playing every note individually. If you remove that part away, and you go on to play the note and its relative third at the same time, you start creating new sounds, and these certainly do sound a lot better. Of course, you cannot expect to play everything that way, but the idea is worth a go. Here is how you would play the thirds in C major scale.

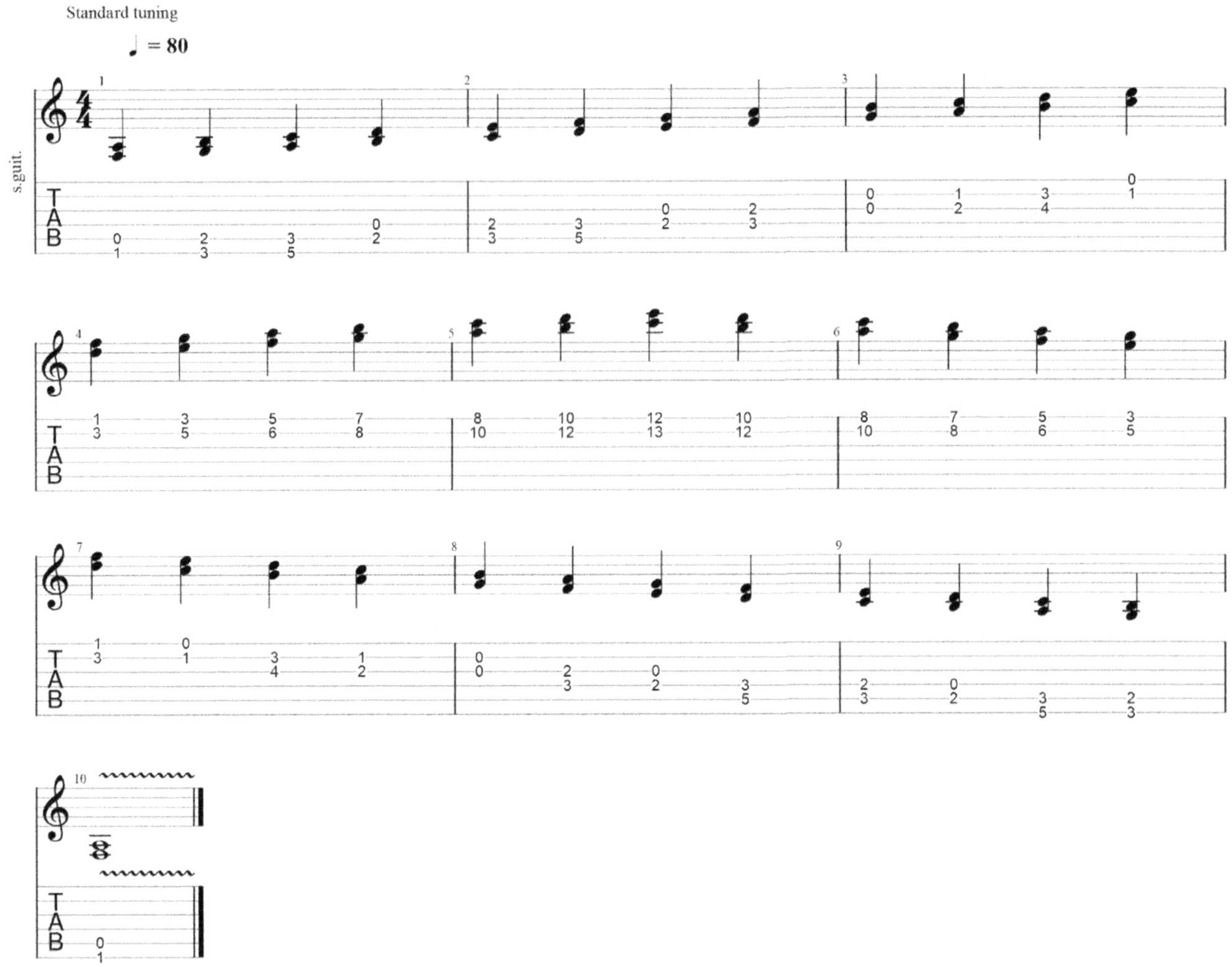

The above is just an example of how you can play a Major scale in thirds. Now, we will also learn how to play a major scale in sixth. Once again, the principle remains the same, but the outcome of playing a major scale in sixth is once again unique.

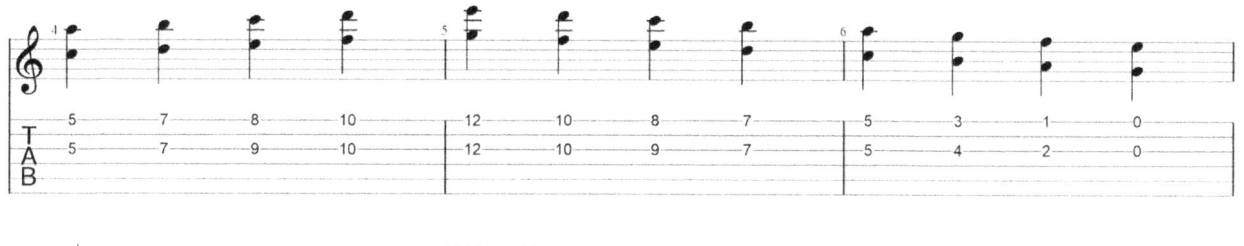

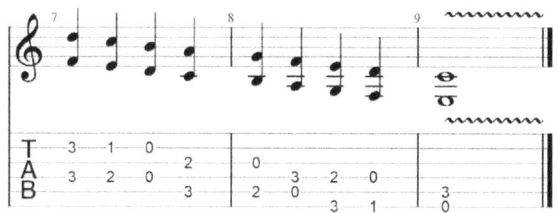

The above is just one of many examples where you will be required to focus more on your execution, get the string skip right, and then play accordingly. For the above, you can now play each of the notes separately, just like you did with the broken thirds. I do understand that alternate picking cannot play two separate strings at the same time, but there is a reason I wanted you to practice that earlier. When you are out on the stage, you may need to improvise, and some of your solos may require you to use both the pick and a finger to play two separate strings at the same time. It comes with practice, which is why you should take all the time you need to gain full command.

Okay. Now that we have our eye in, we know the following:

- ✓ String skipping
- ✓ Alternate picking
- ✓ Thirds and Sixths in major scales

By now, you should also know that timing is essential, not speed. This means that if you secretly decided to dial the tempo down, it's all good. We all have done that, and there is nothing to be ashamed of. Now, however, things will start changing because we will now look at something called a chromatic scale.

If you are a guitarist, and you have been following other great guitarists around the world, chances are that you are already familiar with this guy:

ZAGREB, CROATIA - MAY 16, 2017: Deep Purple guitar player Steve Morse on stage during their The Long Goodbye tour at Arena Zagreb.
© Dariozg

He is none other than the legendary Steve Morse, better known for his mad skills displayed in Deep Purple. He is someone who has single-handedly given chromatic scales the notorious fame it has today.

The chromatic scale is essentially the easiest one to remember. It involves all the 12 notes. This means that if you were to play 'A' chromatic scale, it would start from the fifth string in open position (zero fret) and end on the 11th fret position as the 12th would start the entire scale on a higher octave. This is how it would play and sound like.

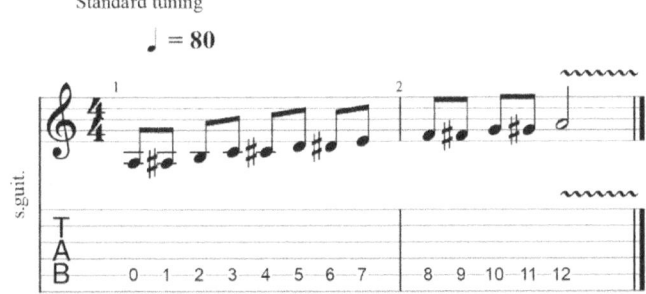

Seems simple, and you even might wonder how on earth can that be used. Well, **Steve Morse** has done just that. Here is a look that is broadly similar to what he would play. It is tough, I grant you that, but forget the sixteenth notes, dial the metronome down, and practice.

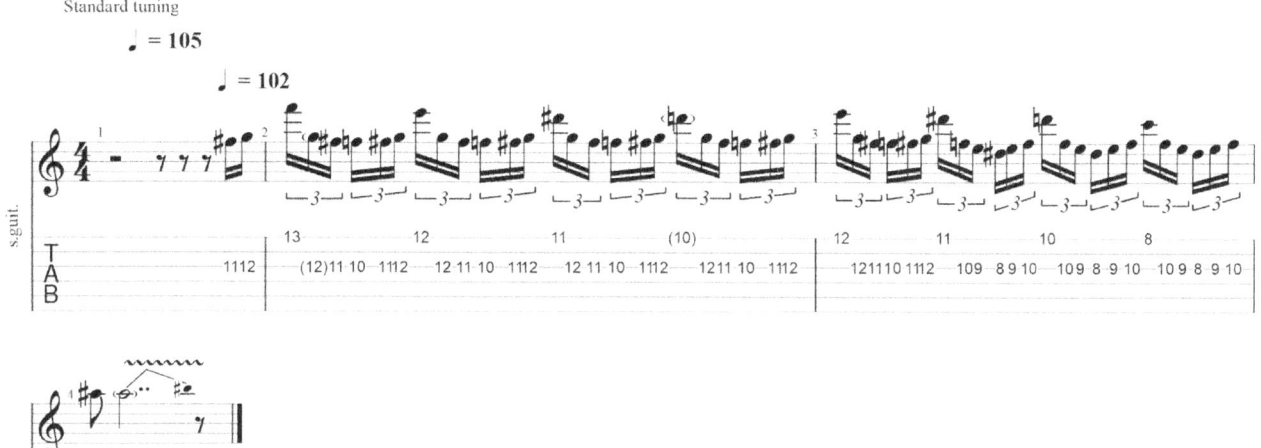

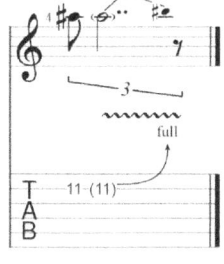

The lick above involves the use of triplets, **D#maj9 sus and D9sus(b2)** chords, bends and rests. However, it goes on to show just how insanely creative Morse is. It is through such licks that he went on to make a name for himself. No wonder why millions of guitarists respect him and praise him for his sheer creativity and skills.

Speaking of chromatic licks, there is one more name that comes to mind, and this guitarist is also one of the most respected guitarists in existence. His name is **John Petrucci**, and you may have heard of him quite a lot.

DENVER JUNE 14: Guitarist John Petrucci of the Progressive Metal band Dream Theater performs in concert June 14, 2010 at the Comfort Dental Amphitheater in Denver, CO. @ TDCPhoto

If you are someone who loves to come up with great lick ideas, or insert fills which sound great, play fantastic, and can easily be incorporated with virtually any key, this lick is for you.

What you see below is an insanely fast lick as all notes are played as sixteenth notes. However, start slow and then gradually pick up the pace once you start feeling comfortable.

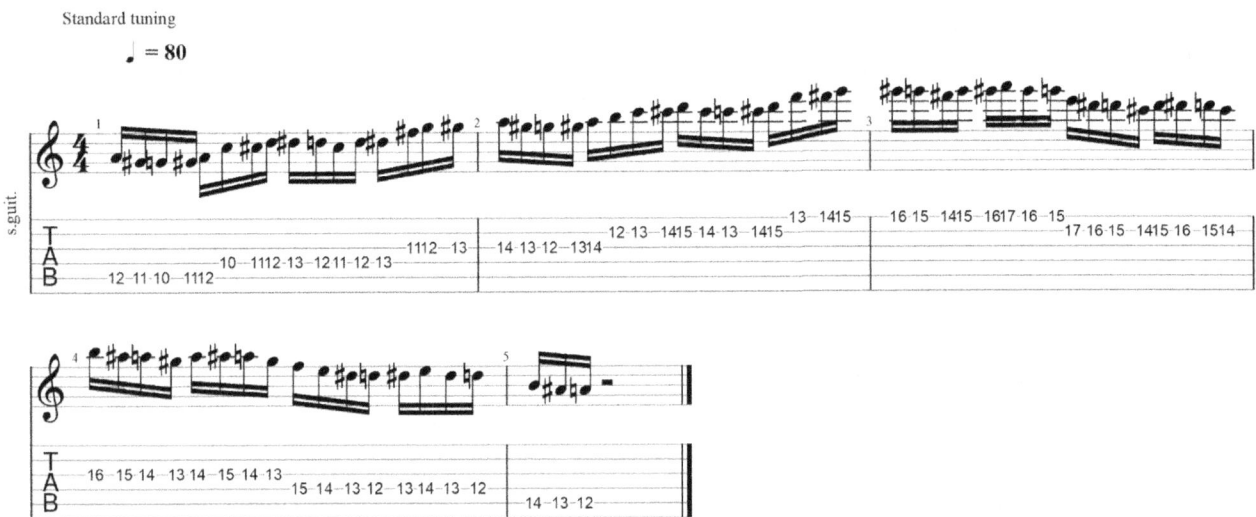

Notice that the above isn't truly chromatic in order. There is quite a lot of shifting and retracing, but the concept remains the same. Every note is played eventually, skipping no half-step or semitone.

Here is another bonus one for you. This one involves the infamous "three-notes" per string approach, and it is yet another classic style of Petrucci.

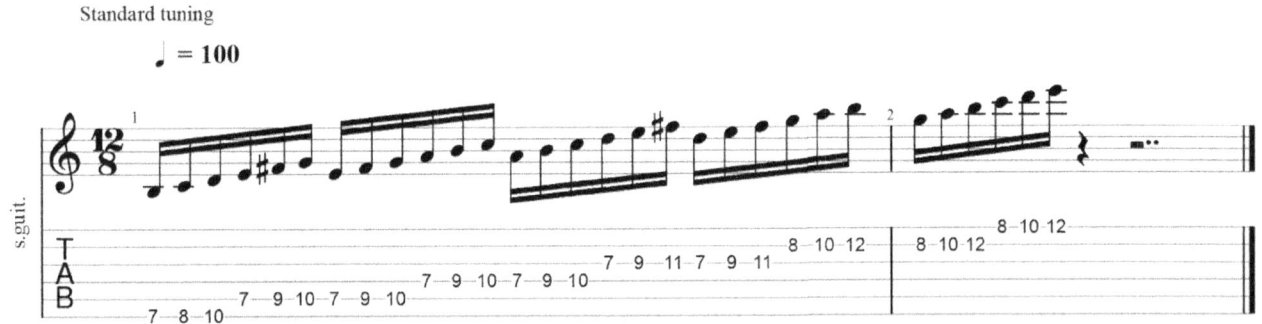

The above uses a **D9 chord**. Notice how sweet it sounds, and how easily your hand glides once you alternate pick your way through the scale. Use a downstroke as your first pick and the rest should come to you naturally. With every string change, you will be using an upstroke. If you fancy the other way around, that is also an option, but not one that many may find comfortable using.

The above only uses three fret positions on every string and they perfectly follow a chord pattern too. You can take the entire pattern to any other starting point, in case the above doesn't fit your song or track. It is a traditional Petrucci style of playing, and can often be used as a great filler in your songs.

Finally, or at least for this chapter, we have one more lick that showcases just how powerful alternate picking is, and how it can easily help us pull off speedy licks in no time. To help you with that, I have found a perfect descending **harmonic E minor** scale in the style of **Yngwie Malmsteen**. It is easy, it is fun, but above all, it is extremely cool to pull off without a glitch.

Alterna2 http://www.alterna2.com, CC BY 2.0 <https://creativecommons.org/licenses/by/2.0>, via Wikimedia Commons

Before We Move Ahead

This chapter has managed to scratch the surface, and I assure you that there is a lot more to learn. However, I am tempted to remind you that this book isn't about how quickly you can go from cover to cover. Your primary objective is to practice everything you come across and move further ahead once you start using the knowledge you have gained so far. Your inner-self should be able to say:

"Hey, you got this!"

If you are still stuck somewhere, be sure to go through the chapter again. Guitar techniques are not rocket science, meaning that anyone with a bit of passion can easily understand what they must do, and how they can go on to further improve their playing. With that said, it is time to move forward and learn how you can use your palm to mute the unnecessary noise and create some dramatic sounds as well. Oh yeah, the good stuff is just around the corner!

CHAPTER 2:

Palm Muting Technique

One fine day, you sit there with your guitar, thinking about what to play. Your thoughts are constantly interrupted by the "weeeeeeee" or the "grrrrr" noise your guitar makes. It's like the guitar having a grumpy day, and not feeling like it wants to be played. Annoying, isn't it? Well, that's where this genius technique of palm muting comes along. Simply place your palm over the strings and the strings stop vibrating. No vibration, no noise — problem solved!

However, if that is the case, what exactly is the 'technique' here? It is an obvious question, and I know that if I was in your position, I'd surely be pondering upon that.

You see, the palm muting may have been an accidental find. I do not know who came up with the technique first, but I'd certainly shake their hand and tell them what a fine job they did by introducing this technique to the world. The palm muting technique quickly went on to become a technique that every guitarist around the world wanted to learn, and they use it all the time.

It is through this technique that you can still continue to play as you mute certain strings. Think about it, you may need to play the D major open chord, and for that you would need to either use your thumb to mute the sixth string, or you can use your palm to gently mute one string while allowing you to play the others. It is much easier, and everyone can do that.

Besides that, the palm muting technique is also used to create that heavy 'chug' sound you often hear in blues, rock, and all kinds of genres which use heavy distorted effects on a guitar. It certainly packs a punch if timed right and executed properly. It also creates a bass effect, and when combined with the drums, it feels sublime.

Take a look at Metallica, Alter Bridge, Guns n Roses, Led Zeppelin, or any band you may have heard of, and all of them use palm muting techniques to play insane riffs, rhythms and licks.

Let's take *Fade to Black* by Metallica as an example. The part where the entire song changes, and builds up towards the finale, a distorted guitar starts with a riff using D and E chords, followed by a palm-muted, fast-paced series of notes played between the riffs. That is done using the palm muting technique. Play it normally and you would never be able to create that dramatic feel.

In this chapter, we will explore just how it is executed, along with some simple exercises and great licks to further help you polish your skills as a guitarist. This technique is a must-have for you, if you truly wish to impress the audience and get them to feel their spine tingling with joy and excitement.

Learning The Technique

First things first, we must acquaint ourselves fully with the technique that is involved. I will not only show you how to use your palm to cut out the excess noise, but I will also show some cool exercises to get you in the flow and teach you how to play notes or chords while muting the same.

> **SIDE NOTE:** *If you are using an acoustic guitar, do not worry. The same principles apply for you as well. You can use palm muting to create rhythmic patterns or add in some much-needed drama to the music.*

Have a look at the picture below and try to pay close attention to what is going on.

Yes, the guitar looks gorgeous, and those shiny knobs, neck, fretboard, it is all too tempting, but that isn't what we are here to focus on. See that palm? It is placed right over the sixth, fifth and fourth strings. Effectively, it is muting them. That is exactly how you execute palm-muting.

The technique is extremely simple but how you end up using that to further increase your skills is quite a different ball game altogether. Here is a quick exercise for you:

Set the metronome to 90 bpm, and begin by using a downstroke to play a complete chord. You can play any chord of your choosing. The idea is to play one stroke the first beat, mute for the second beat (silencing the already sustaining chord you played just moments ago), then playing the chord once again on the third beat and then repeating the above.

Once you get the hang of the above, start by mixing things up a little. Now, instead of just muting, use the technique to create a 'chuggy' sound and play the chord on alternate beats while using the technique.

Beat one: Play Clean

Beat two: Play muted

Beat three: Play Clean

Beat four: Play Muted

Of course, you are free to improvise and change the sequence as you please. Once you are ready, we will move ahead.

To further help you explain the concept, and to get those creative ideas flowing, here is an exercise I normally suggest newbies try out. It helps in understanding more complex rhythm patterns, uses the alternate picking, and teaches how to keep pace with the tempo. Please note, we are using "Power Chords" for the exercise. If you do not know what those are, they are essentially played using three strings only while muting the others. They are used by almost every single guitarist I know of.

The above shows a simple pattern. To further explain how the above works, let's go over this step by step.

1. Begin by playing the first power chord 'E5'.

2. Using alternate picking, we will play the chord, then palm mute (PM) and play, followed by another PM and play, and then restart the loop. It should look like this: Play>PM>PM>Play>PM>PM>Play>PM>PM

3. After the above, the last three instances are to be plate as two strokes. The last two are interlinked, or sustained, meaning that you would only need to strike the first time and let it ring until it is time to change your chord.

4. Follow the same pattern for all except the last one.

Throughout the PM and play, use your palm to gently mute the strings and then play those muted strings with a more powerful stroke. Remember, muted strings would need more force than usual in order to create any meaningful sound.

Take it slow, if the above seems to be a little too fast for your liking. You can always add in any other power chords, or change the sequence. I highly encourage you to try and find your own rhythmic patterns using the palm muting technique. You'd be surprised how different and impactful your chords would sound like when you use this technique.

Personally, I love using palm muting technique, specifically just before changing a chord, just to give that classical 'chug-a-chug' sound. I honestly feel like a rockstar, or maybe that's just me being odd.

Here is one that I decided to present to you. It involves some power chords, and it also uses some individual notes. Try this one out and see if you can work your way around using palm mute for the rhythms, and playing the remainder of the notes clean.

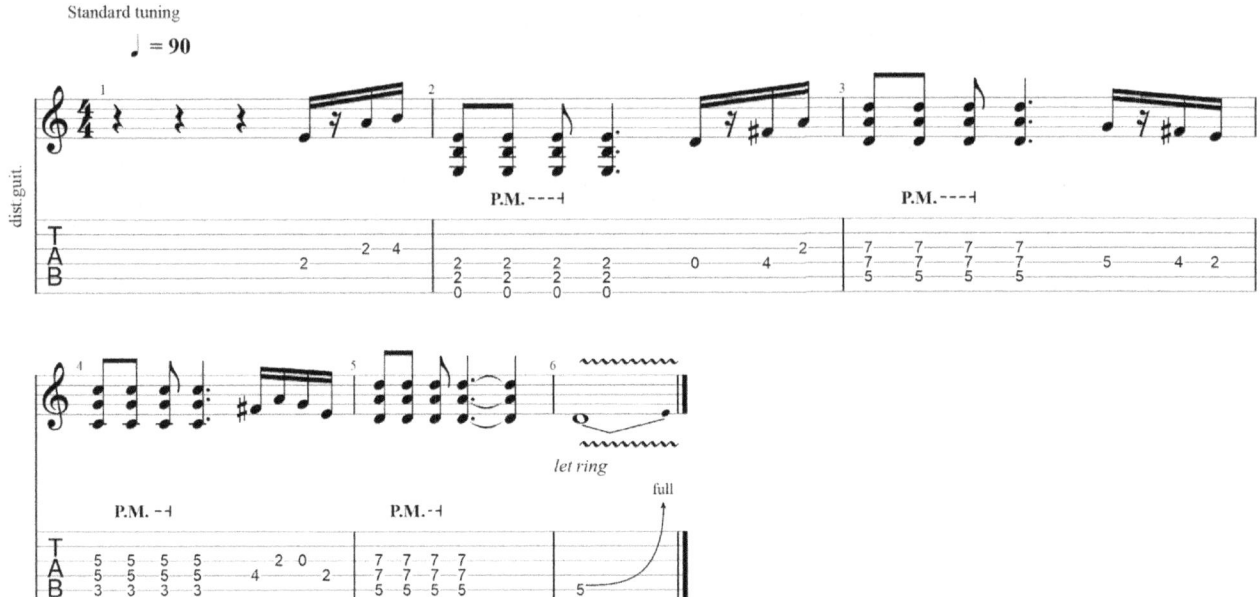

I created this one quite some time ago when I was learning my way around the palm muting technique. Feel free to improve the above, improvise, or modify to whatever you feel like. The above piece allows you to use the bending technique, rests, palm muting, and it also helps you to quickly navigate through the fretboard and get back on the rhythm, all without missing the beats. If you were able to do this in the first go, and that too without missing out on any beat, or striking any note or chord when it wasn't supposed to, what are you doing here? You should be out wowing the crowds!

Now that you have your eye in, let's learn a little more about how you can improve your palm muting technique and do even better.

Left-Right Sync

One of the biggest hurdles we guitarists face is managing the left-hand, right-hand synchronization. Get that wrong and all hell breaks loose. Things aren't any different for us when we intend to use the palm muting technique either.

So far, I have taught you on how to use your palm to mute strings. This, of course, is the right hand (the one with the plectrum or pick). What about the left hand?

"Umm... Isn't that responsible for holding the fret positions?"

Well, yes and no. Yes, as that is a no-brainer, however, what's interesting is the fact that you can do a lot more than just press on fret positions and strings with your left hand and the fingers involved. You can actually use your left hand to further strengthen the synchronization, especially when you are aiming to do a bit of palm muting.

Take the power chords exercise I gave you initially. When you are holding the chord position, don't keep pressing on the notes while you use the other hand to mute them. If you loosen up your grip slightly, you can further amp up the muting effect. Try it yourself. Play out the E5 power chord four times. The first time, do not let go of the notes at all, and only use your right hand to mute the strings between each stroke of pick. Play using the sentence shown below:

One — and a — Two — and a — Three — and a — Four

For each number, play the chord, and for the middle parts, mute the strings. You will soon find out that it is slightly uncomfortable, and can cause confusion when you try to mute the strings only using the right hand. Now, play the same thing once again. This time, however, play and then mute using the palm with the right hand, and loosening up your grip but still touching the strings with your left hand. Now, your mind finds it easier because it no longer needs to push out two separate messages at the same time. It sends out the command 'mute' and both your hands do the job instantly.

You can use this technique to further help you create muting effects when you are using your right hand to strum chords, and you know you cannot afford to rest your right hand. Simply loosen the grip to create the effect, strike at the same time to amplify the 'chug' sound, and then apply pressure once again to resume the normal notes.

Position Matters

While you can place your palm almost anywhere to mute the string, it is worth noting that your position of the palm does matter and changes how the output would sound like.

If you are someone who is looking to create a more sustained muted sound, you should use your palm and place it just over the bridge of the guitar. On the other hand, if you were to place your palm over the neck pickup, you would find that the strings almost instantly die out, leaving virtually no sustain or resonance of any kind. The sweet spot, for most guitarists, is right in the middle.

This is not a mandatory rule that you should always follow. Feel free to find which position works best for you. There may be instances where you will want to use shorter sustains, and for that you would move closer to the neck pickup.

Tweaking The Effect

Using your tone knobs and pickup selector, you can dramatically change the way your guitar sounds when you use the palm muting technique. You can either crank up the tone all the way to create a brighter 'chug' or you can dial it down and choose the neck pickup to create a more darker sound. The possibilities are numerous, if not limitless.

The best practice is to try out each of these settings, tweak them a little until you have come across one that suits most of your needs perfectly well. As an added bonus tip, I would recommend writing down the settings somewhere, for future references. Trust me, you do not wish to come across a situation where you "did something" and when you really need it, you cannot recall what it was.

Gain Settings

One of the most obvious questions on everyone's mind is this:

How much gain should I use to compliment the palm muting technique?

To be honest, it completely depends on the kind of music you play. Earlier in the book, I mentioned Metallica. If you go back in time and play their older soundtracks, you would identify that they relied on very high gains.

Metallica made it popular for the world to use such a high gain. People would often dial the gain or overdrive all the way to 11 (in other words, maximum). That was them when they were young. This does not mean that you need all of the gain you can get from your amp or pedals.

You have the room to experiment, but the general rule of thumb is that you need sufficient gain in order to pull off quality dampened sounds.

If you are using equalizers (EQ), be sure to bring up the mid-tones higher to further amplify the heavy damp sounds created when using this technique.

Fret-Wraps

Some may call these as tools to cheat, but I kind of like the idea of having a fret-wrap around the nut region of the neck. For those who may not know what a fret-wrap is, it is essentially a piece of fabric that is designed to mute the strings or the excess noise you occasionally get from the nut of the guitar. You simply tie it around the nute region, and the noise automatically eliminates, allowing you to focus on your playing and not worry about the noises.

Another advantage is that you can slide these down to any fret position, and they will effectively mute all the strings save the ones you are playing on. The accidental hits or resonance would no longer be a cause of concern to you, especially if you are playing split chords.

With that said, however, they do have some downsides. The biggest downside is the fact that they can often get in the way of a guitarist, especially when playing live or recording. You will need to manually adjust them every time you use them. This means that you will have to let go of the notes, readjust the position of the wrap and then go back to what you were doing, and that is a waste of energy and time. The other problem is that some guitarists consider this as cheating, and it is often frowned upon by professionals. This would imply that you are someone who just doesn't know how to mute the strings and that you have to rely on 'help' to get the job done.

As for me, I don't consider them as an essential, but they are certainly nice to have lying around. You never know when you might need them. If you can learn how to use them properly, they can certainly help you create better palm muting results, allowing you to further explore more creative ideas, without running into the excess noise problems.

Practicing Palm Muting

For this exercise, I would recommend using some kind of software through which you can record a rhythm track for a guitar. You can then use that as a backtrack and play along. Alternatively, you can ask one of your friends to fill in the part and play the rhythms while you practice the solos. Both the parts contain simple palm-muting techniques, and are easy to follow.

This is actually a pretty good way to practice. It is only natural that when you are practicing using a backtrack, you will naturally be tempted to improvise and do something out of the ordinary. This is how many great songs are found, composed, and made, which is why it is necessary that you never let your inner instincts and creativity die out. Never be ashamed of trying something that may or may not sound nice. It is through various trials and errors that you finally come across a find that is worth the efforts and patience.

Now, let us make things a little more difficult. I promise, it isn't that hard, but it is a little trickier. For the next exercise, we will be using only three

notes on each string to create a lick. You are more than welcome to create your own, or you can always begin by exploring the one below and then take it from there.

It is simple, it is exquisite, and the best part is that you can always use it from any other starting position, just to make it sound more natural to your choice of key. The above involves the use of PM, bending (both half-step and full-step), and alternate picking.

Another thing that you covered beautifully here was the fact that you used PM in both the directions. You used it when scaling up, and you used the same when coming back down. I will use the same concept to further instill confidence in you and your playing.

Using the C Major scale, and the PM technique, you should be able to play this with relative ease.

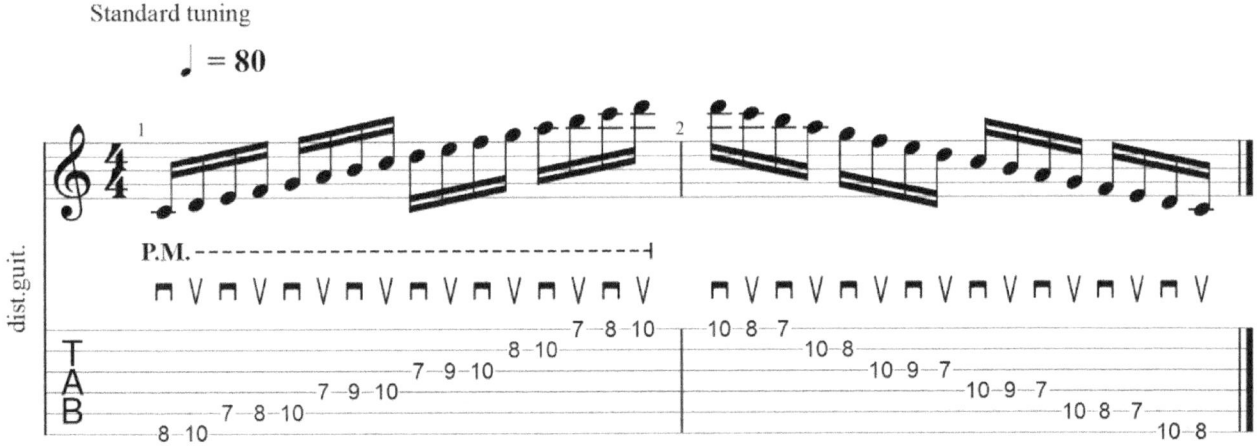

Take your time because muting the first and second strings can at times be a bit tricky. You will also notice that they create a weaker sound, one that can fade more easily as compared to the more bulkier strings. Once you are able to get the sound you need, reverse the pattern and ascend playing the notes and descend while using PM.

Finally, here is one lick that you should certainly get to know, learn and practice. It uses the PM technique, and allows you to shred some really cool entry/exit fills. This uses A minor Pentatonic, but you can always incorporate it in other scales easily by shifting the pattern to relevant fret positions. The pattern, overall, would remain the same.

The slash you see just before the note is called a slide. It is one of the most essential techniques in existence. In the above, the "/" shows that you need to slide from some position prior to the note itself. So for "/7" you can begin your slide from the fifth fret and then make your way to the seventh fret and continue.

Well, earlier I did say 'finally' but now I am thinking that I am feeling generous. Therefore, as a guitarist to another guitarist, I will provide you

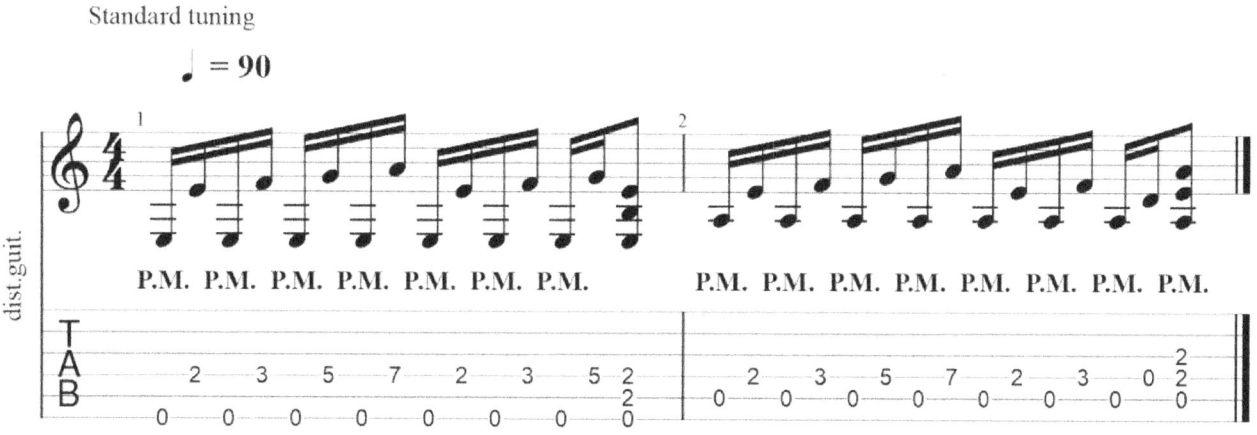

with four more licks you can practice and use, all to further master the ability to palm mute. I hope you are as ready as I am. Let's get going.

Well, this brings us to the end of this chapter, but the fun has not stopped. I promise you that we have a lot of exciting stuff waiting right around the corner. We will be learning a lot about how you can use something called 'vibrato' that not only makes the note feel more natural and humanly, but it also adds flair and style to the playing. The good thing is that you have already used it (those curvy lines in the scores above). With that said, let's dive into the world of vibrato and find out what's what, and why people are often obsessed with these.

CHAPTER 3:

Vibrato

Have you often heard various singers sustaining their notes longer and adding a bit of flair by magically vibrating their note? There was a time that this technique was only limited to those who played along with orchestras or were renowned opera singers. With time, people started gaining knowledge about this incredible technique.

Whether singers or guitarists, we all face one situation where we need to strike and hold a note for longer durations, even if that 'longer' duration is just a second. This sustained note stands out because the rest of the notes are generally shorter and take half or even less as much time to play. This, then, poses a problem: How on earth are we supposed to hold a note or two for that long without making it sound monotonous or repetitive?

Fortunately, someone back in the day came up with the idea of introducing vibrato to the world of guitars, and it worked like a charm. The world welcomed the sweet sounds of vibrato with open arms, and the rest is just history. Today, vibrato is seen as one of the most sought after skills in the business. It may seem straight and simple, but there are far too many ways one can use vibrato creatively, and not all of them are worth the efforts. It takes a special sense of music to figure out what kind of vibrato would suit, and where.

In our previous chapter, where we learned palm muting, I introduced many licks which involved the use of the vibrato technique. Most of them took place right at the end, especially to sustain the note and give it that natural, human-like feel as the note fades out. There were some instances where I also used vibrato in the middle, to act more like a pivotal point, or to emphasize on a specific note without increasing the duration itself. This goes to show that vibrato is versatile, and can be used in a variety of ways to suit the need.

While virtually every guitarist uses the vibrato technique, there are some who stand out as the grand masters. These are legends who have gone on to redefine the use of vibrato and have pushed the creative edge further, quite literally exploring uncharted creativity and pioneering the variations and techniques. Some of these legends include:

Apart from the above two, you may have also heard of Greg Howe, and Allan Holdsworth. All of these are maestros at their traits, especially Steve Vai.

Personally speaking, we literally do not even know an ounce of playing guitars if we start comparing ourselves with the way Steve Vai plays. Insane or mad would be words which would not even begin to describe what he is capable of. Using vibrato, the whammy bar, and his iconic tapping skills, he quite literally makes the guitar scream like a horse. I am not exaggerating here at all, and if you do not believe me, go ahead and check out his *Bad Horsie* soundtrack to understand just how incredibly… incredible he is.

English band Queen performs during the concert in Hong Kong, China, 28 September 2016   @ ChinaImages

Brian May

Anyways, I am not here to discuss his skills, but I am certainly here to talk you through the skill called vibrato. This chapter will provide you with a few great licks, exercises, and the friendly "how to" to ensure everyone knows what they need to do.

> **SIDE-NOTE:** *Since we are progressing so well, I will be providing you with more difficult licks from here on out. Do not be afraid to test your skills and push yourself to the max. It is through failure and learning that you will truly become great.*

Vibrating The Daylight Out of the Note

Let us get the trickier bits out first. There are a few ways vibrato works. These include:

1. Vertical vibrato

2. Horizontal vibrato

3. Circular vibrato

4. Gre Howe esque vibrato

Each of these types of vibrato essentially does the same thing, but their outputs are dramatically different, or at least to those who pay close attention to the notes. While the first two techniques are more commonly used, the third and fourth techniques require a lot of practice to master, but once done, can produce some of the most breath-taking results.

I will take you through each one of these using simple exercises, to illustrate just how we pull these off and how we are able to produce the kind of sounds we require.

Vertical Vibrato

This is one of the most basic ones out there. However, just because it is the first kind of vibrato everyone learns does not mean that it is useless at all. Believe it or not, it is still one of the most respected techniques in existence, and if you can manage to master this alone, you may not need to worry about learning the rest either.

The vertical vibrato is pretty much like the bend technique. From the term 'vertical' it is easy to understand that this type of vibrato uses the lateral movement to create the effect. However, when you go on to perform this, you will need to ensure that you do not bend the string too high or too low (yes, bends go down as well). If you do that, you would end up executing the bend technique, and that may alter the pitch of the note you intended to play.

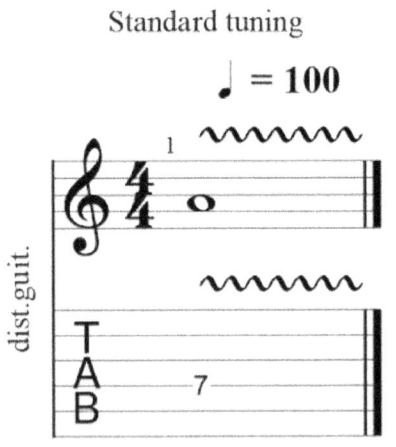

To execute a vertical vibrato, use a metronome. and play any note, say seventh fret on the fourth string. Now, as you play the note, bend the note slightly in an up-and-down motion. You will start hearing the vibrating effect or vibrato.

Timing your vibrato right is essential as it helps highlight the note and add in expression to the music. Besides that, another important aspect is to match the up-and-down motion with the tempo. Since you will be doing the action quickly, it is a good idea to use a metronome and start working on how you can match the temp and still pull off incredible vibratos.

The vertical vibratos have superiority over horizontal vibratos. The biggest advantage is the fact that whether you bend the string up or down, the note will still play on the same pitch. By alternating the movement, you end up creating a moving sound.

The vertical vibrato can be further divided into four unique types. These are:

- Finger vibrato
- Whole-hand vibrato
- Wrist vibrato
- Arm vibrato

The finger vibrato can be performed by keeping your thumb at the back of the neck and then using the fingers to pull off the vibrato movement. If you place your thumb on top of the neck, and then try to pull off a vibrato, you would end up using the wrist to create that effect.

In some cases, you may be tempted to keep your thumb behind the neck, and use something other than finger vibrato. For that, use your hand from the wrist to create an up and down motion while playing a note. This is called "whole-hand" vibrato.

Finally, you have the arm/elbow vibrato, and this is one of the toughest to control. It is easy to lose control of the string or the neck when performing this, which is why I would not suggest you do worry about using this technique (at least for now).

The example below shows multiple uses of vibrato. The technique, of course, is yours to choose. Since we are doing the vertical vibrato, use any of the variations, as mentioned above, to execute these.

The thing to notice here is that I moved the string up and down four times in quick succession, and that too while matching the tempo of the metronome. In the last bar, I halved the number of fluctuations as I knew it was practically impossible to do four and still be able to match the tempo.

The vertical vibrato technique is used by many great artists, and if you wish to fully explore its potential, tune into *Comfortably Numb* by Pink Floyd, or *Fade to Black* by Metallica. All of these great songs go on to show just how powerful the technique is, and just how much expressions are added just by a simple technique.

Now, I will provide you another lick, but this time, I will be both the slower and the faster vibrato effects. See if you can learn how to play and identify fast and slow vibrato. The following uses an E natural minor pentatonic scale.

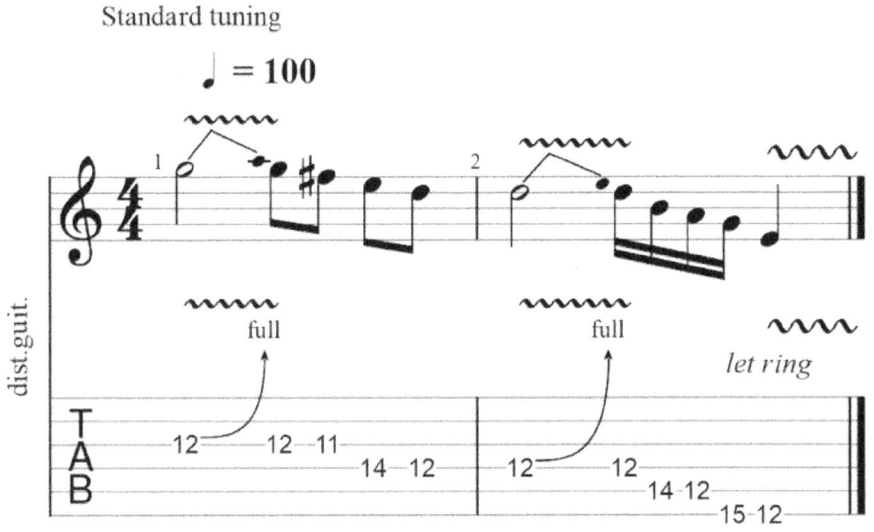

In this example, you can see the use of both slow and fast vibratos. The one in the end is a slower one. It is quite obvious that when you use the slower vibrato, it will be more prominent, and it will result in moving sound which almost changes pitch. Vocalists across the globe use slower vibratos commonly, especially if they are to hold a note longer. In this instance, I let the last note ring until it fades. Naturally, the note might have died earlier, but owing to the vibrato, I was able to sustain the note for a longer duration.

You may have also noticed that I have used two instances where I bend the string instead of playing the specific note on its relative position. I will be talking a lot about bending in a future chapter to further highlight its importance and technicalities.

Horizontal Vibrato

Unlike the vertical or lateral vibrato, the horizontal vibrato uses horizontal movement to create the vibrato effect. It is also a powerful trick to have up your sleeve, and it certainly pays off well, if timed right and executed perfectly.

The horizontal vibrato does have its limitation, and there is none bigger than the fact that the pitch of the note can change the second you move your finger a little too much. Slide it further back, and you end up playing the previous fret, and the story remains the same if you move towards the next fret. Unlike the vertical vibrato, this takes time and practice to master.

Before jumping into the lick, let me teach you how to perform this technique.

1. Choose a note and play it.

2. As it rings, slide the finger within the fret back and forth.

That's it! See? It wasn't exactly hard, was it? Now, try and play four half notes (one note per two beats) on any bpm you like. Use the newly learned technique to sustain the note and move the finger about in a rhythmic fashion, matching the tempo of the metronome. Just like with notes, you can either slide left and right once every 'click' or four times, it's completely up to you. See how simple movement creates the same result as the lateral vibrato we learned earlier? Good. Let's move on to the exercises then.

The following two licks are good starting points to get in the zone and practice the horizontal vibrato.

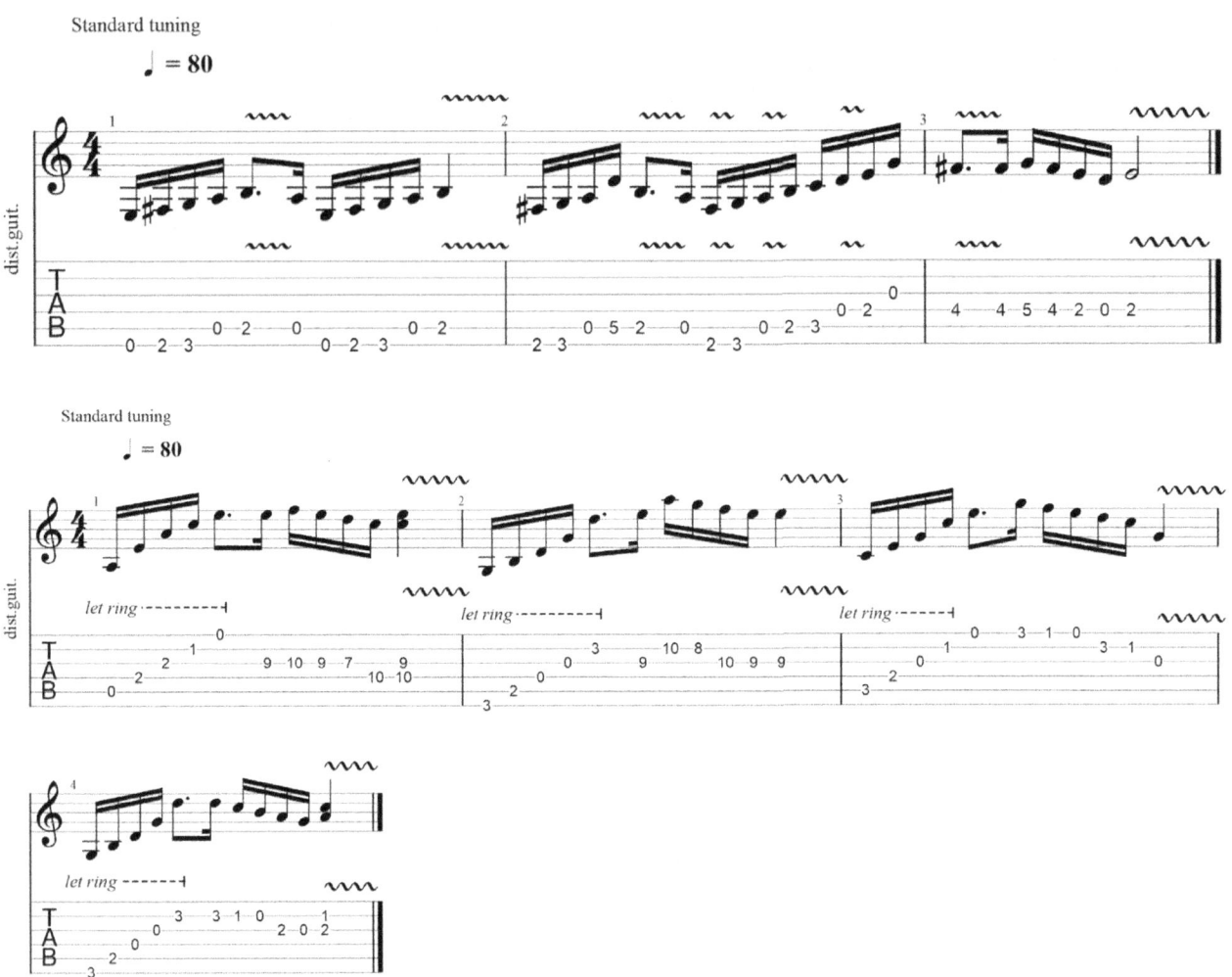

Hopefully, the above two should keep you engaged rather well. The technique is not easy, but it isn't exactly tough either. Once again, patience is key. Learn to execute it properly so that the modulating sound speaks as if it were a human note.

Circular Vibrato

Okay, I will be fairly honest with you here. This one is not at all easy to master. I have only seen a select few legendary guitarists actually use this technique, which further goes to show that this technique is hard to master, and even harder to use with varying tempos and beats.

Of course, Satriani, Vai, Petrucci, are icons in the business. This means that they occasionally show the world why they are so phenomenally successful through a variety of techniques which to us feeble minded guitarists seem unfathomable. The circular vibrato is one of them.

Executing the motion is easy, but maintaining that circular motion, while ensuring that you do not skip a fret or bend the string too high, and carry out the motion that compliments the bpm count, that's a lot of work.

The circular vibrato is more of a hybrid, and it was immortalized by Steve Vai himself. Unlike the lateral one, where you had to bend the string up and down, or the horizontal one, where you could only move side to side, the circular motion gives you the best of these two worlds combined into one swift move.

There is no rule of thumb that says "You must only use circular vibrato in clockwise movement" or even the opposite. It is completely up to you on how you decide to play it.

With the kind of motion this special technique uses, you can actually use vibrato for more than two notes. You can play chords and still use the circular vibrato, and that is exactly what **Steve Vai** has shown time and again in his live performances.

Start by picking a note, and then pushing the string and move your finger with the string in a circular formation. Remember, do

Rio de Janeiro, Brazil, June 6, 2019.Guitarist Steve Vai during his show at the Rio Montreux Jazz Festival at the Pier de la Plaza Mau in the city of Rio de Janeiro. @ A.Paes

not push the string too high or low, or slide your finger across the fret as there are still chances you may end up doing that, causing you to play an unnatural note. Through the use of circular vibrato, your intonation problem is kept in check, most of the time.

The circular motion brings warmth to the note while ensuring sustain and vibrato effects, all of which makes it unique and a worthy skill to learn. To get started, here is a simple exercise. It does not involve any technicalities except one; you are only supposed to strike the string once and then use the circular vibrato to sustain the note, slide to the next ones, do the same until the entire section finishes.

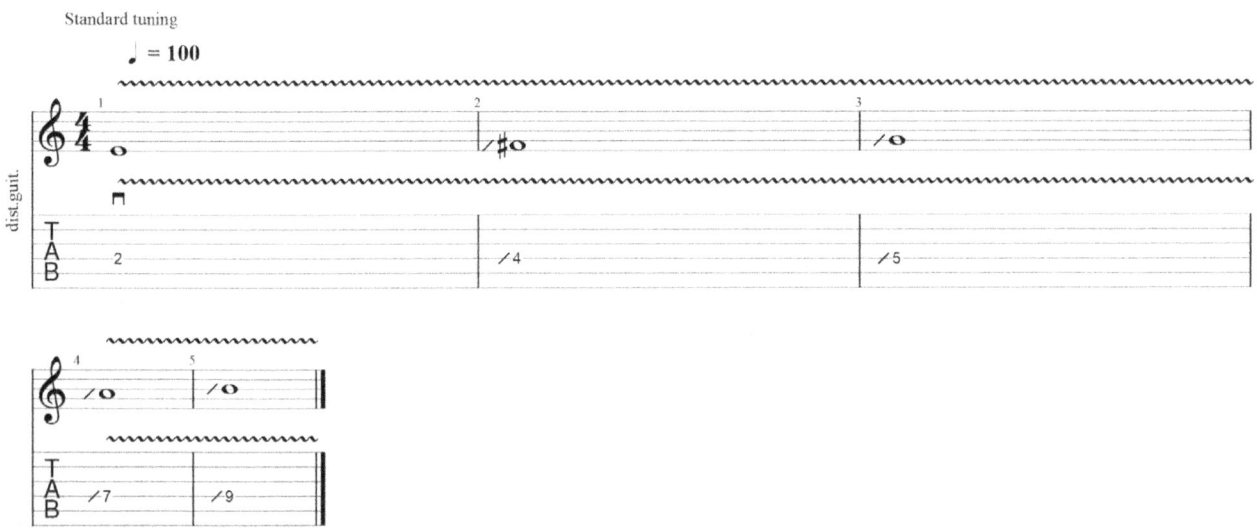

This is a lot harder than it looks. For acoustic guitar players, you may not be able to sustain the notes that long, and for that case, you can trim down the duration to suit the maximum sustain on your strings.

Hopefully, you were able to do the above, and since you did, bravo! This instills confidence in me that I can now provide you with slightly more advanced licks.

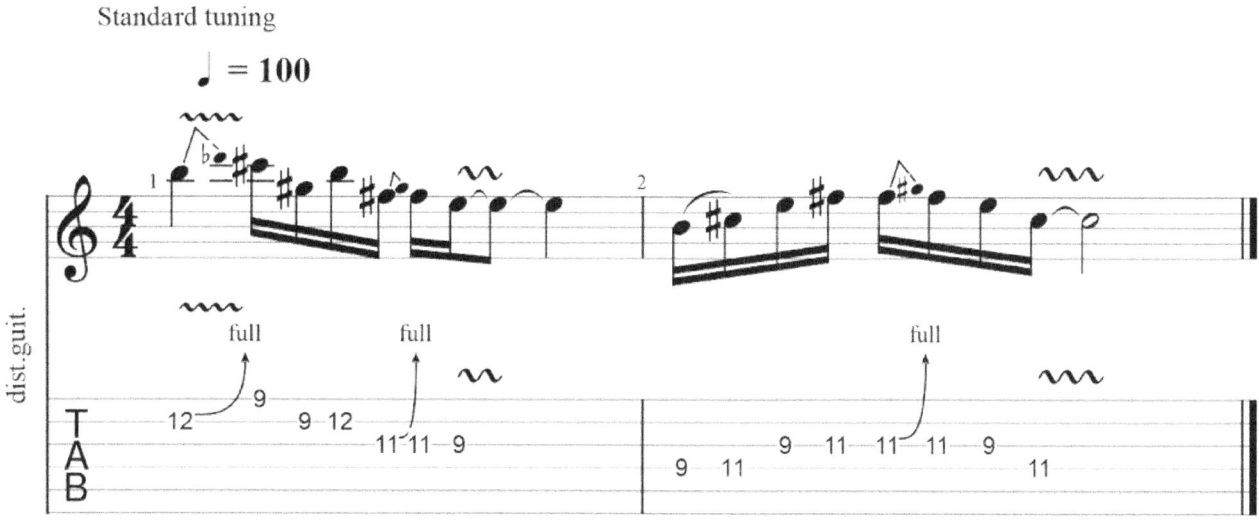

The above is a versatile lick. It uses E major scale, and I am quite fond of using this occasionally.

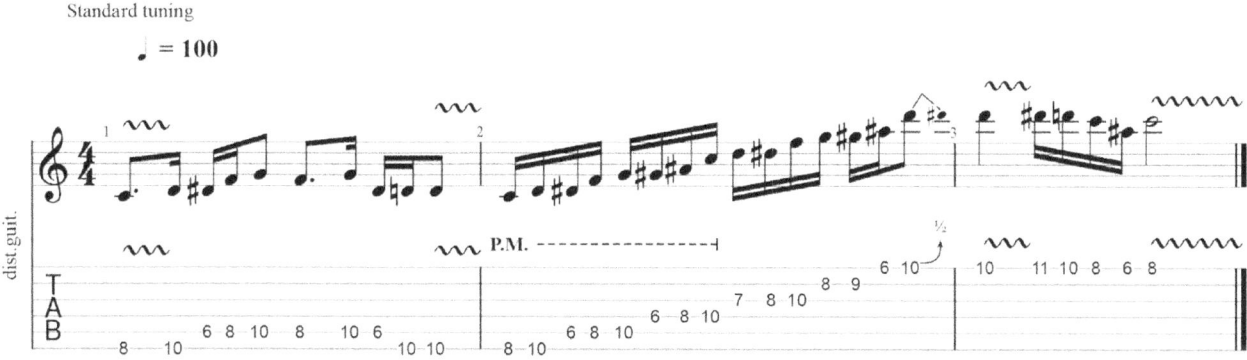

The above uses **C minor**. This was slightly different because it involves quicker circular motions, and involves palm muting and playing a complete scale. However this exercise does teach you how to switch from the circular vibrato to continue playing, and then use the same technique again on thinner strings. You would find it harder to play a circular vibrato note on the first string as it would quite literally have you go under the neck. Take your time to practice this, and soon you should be able to do this with relative ease, and even impress others around you instantly.

Greg Howe Esque Vibrato

"Howe what?"

I had the same reaction the first time I came across the name. Greg Howe is a renowned guitarist, known for displaying his extreme technical skills with the guitars. Along the way, he came up with a revolutionary new technique to create stunning vibrato effects. The technique requires him to break the rules and think out of the box, and it is easy to see how he does that.

Theoretically speaking, this technique is almost the same as the horizontal vibrato. The major difference is that where the horizontal one is limited within the confines of the specific fret position, this breaks that by sliding to the next and then towards the previous, all in extremely swift motion. It is safe to say that it is done so fast that it is quite literally an optical illusion for many.

Speed, for this technique, is essential. It is so because doing this technique with a slower approach would reveal the off notes loud and clear. It needs to be done as fast as possible, all without losing control of your slide, and as a result you get a dramatic vibrato effect.

Below is a lick inspired from Howe's work. Right at the end, try and give this technique a go. Slide your finger, while applying pressure to the string, and move it to the next fret, back to the original, to the one before the actual fret, and back to the original. All of this must be done quickly, and without breaking the tempo. Ideally, try and aim for four movements for every beat (start with 80 bpm to give yourself a chance).

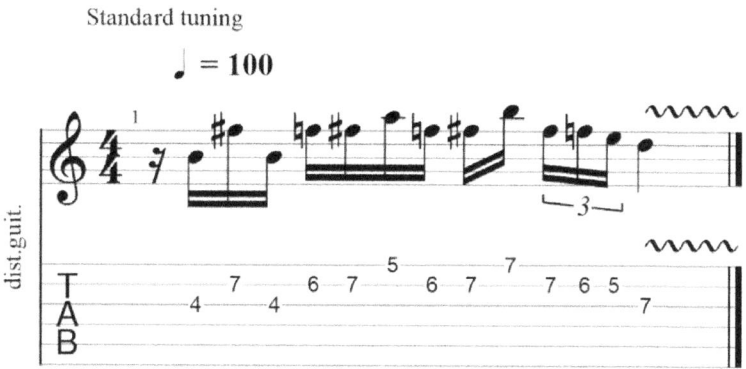

Played in **D Major.**

Once you are comfortable with the concept, try and play the same using the original 100 bpm. Consider it as a challenge, but I assure you, it is well worth the efforts. Oh, and it uses D major (D major ionian, in case you're wondering).

And that about wraps up this chapter. Of course, there is a lot that you have learned, and you may need some time to process all the knowledge, practice it and start applying it. Don't worry, I ain't going anywhere. I will be right

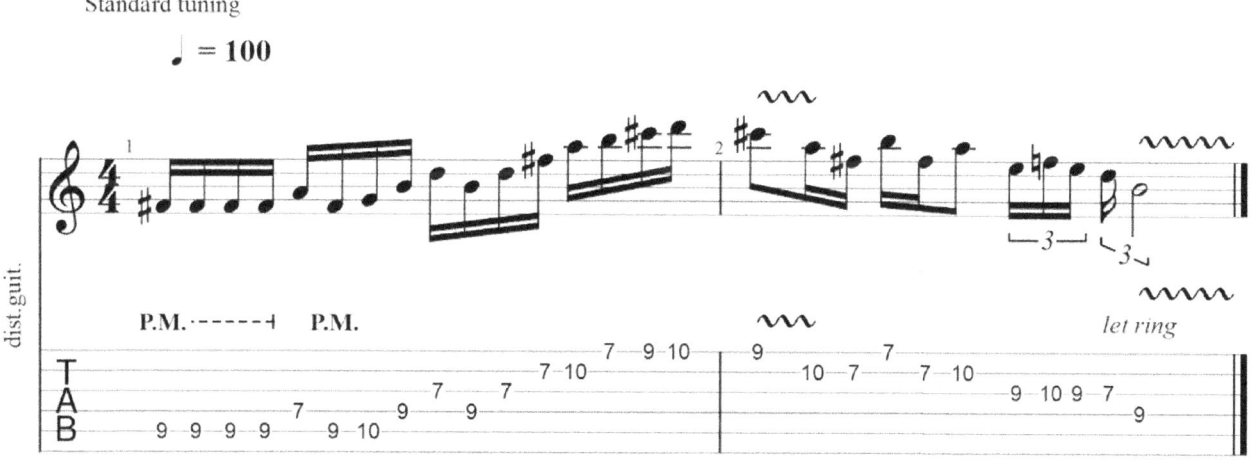

here, waiting for you to feel confident enough before moving on to the next chapter, and that is where we will be learning all about Legato, and how that is different from vibrato.

CHAPTER 4:

Legato

Quite often, I see people confusing Legato with vibrato, and I am often questioning myself, "Why? Why would people think that these two are the same?" It took me quite a long time before I was able to figure out the obvious answer.

"They just don't know it yet."

While they may sound like they are related, the fact is that vibrato and legato are poles apart. Each one of these two techniques differ in purpose, quality, output and style of execution.

To give you a better idea, have a look at **Joe Satriani, Tom Quayle, Tim Miller** or **Allan Holdsworth.** You will note that they often start picking a single note and then they continue to play notes in succession without actually picking most of them. That is what a legato is. It is a technique that incorporates the combination of hammer-on and pull-off techniques, combined together to deliver world-class licks.

They are exquisite to practice, and even more fun to perform. In the most basic terms, they are the stuff of every guitarist's dream. To be able to stand on a stage, perform a song, and then finish it off with a lick in style, that is what a legato can do for you with ease and finesse.

Therefore, in this chapter, we will be looking into how legato is performed, and how you and I can apply legato to our licks. This chapter will be fun, and it will teach you not one, not two, but three unique techniques, so pay close attention.

Hammers and Pulls

Let's talk about the hammer-on technique first. It is one of the two core components which go on to make legato.

Imagine holding a hammer and a nail. Your job is to use the hammer to nail the nail into something, and to do that, all you need is to strike the nail using the hammer. In roughly the same manner, now imagine holding the fifth fret on any string using the index finger. Next, you want to play the seventh fret using the ring finger, but without using the pick. To do that, your seventh fret becomes the nail, and your ring finger becomes the hammer. Put two and two together, and you will immediately know what you need to do next. With some force, strike the seventh fret with your ring finger, and the guitar will play the sound immediately. What happened wasn't exactly magic, but it was what we guitarist call a hammer-on. You hammered on the seventh fret, and as a result, it created music.

Now, let's assume you are on the seventh fret, and you are using your ring finger. You want to play the fifth fret next, and as before, you do not wish to attack the string with a pick. You could try and strike the fifth fret, but that would not change anything because you are still holding on to the seventh fret.

"Perhaps I should let go and then strike."

Well, that is one way, but that would once again be a hammer-on. To do this effortlessly, we use a technique called pull-off. With your ring finger holding the note on the seventh fret, place your index finger on the target fret and press it. Now, pick the seventh note with a pick, and once you hear the sound, pull the string off in a swift motion and let it go while still holding the fifth fret with your index finger. What you will hear now is the sound of the fifth fret being played, hence confirming that you successfully performed a pull off.

It is important to understand that legato isn't only about hammer-ons and pull-offs either. The main purpose is actually to create a series of successive notes, inter-related to each other and executed in a smooth manner, creating an array of wonderful, short and sweet notes. A lot of people tend to get that part wrong, which is why they either overdo the job or mess things up in some other way. There is no point in playing a series of notes every single time. Legato is to be used when you really wish to add some flair or create a build-up to something bigger, such as a lead, bridge or the outro.

Of course, all of this is easier said than done, which is why I am going to give you a simple exercise involving hammer on and pull off. Try and work your way through this before proceeding onwards.

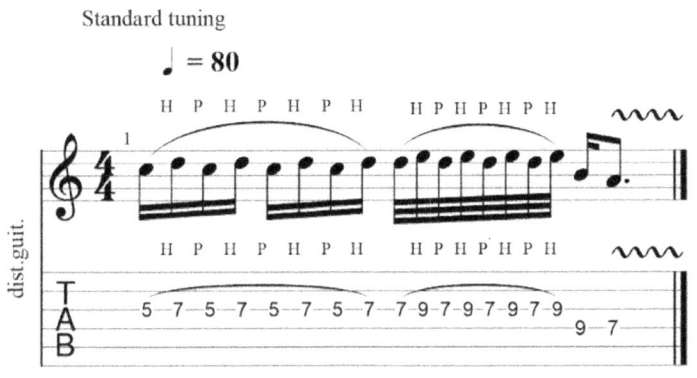

I have dialed the bpm down for this, in case you are someone who has just started exploring the world of hammer-ons and pull-offs. In the above example, we begin by playing the first note using our pick. You can use a downward stroke or an upward, it doesn't matter. Once that is executed, you will carry on playing the 'H' and 'P' notes until the end of the eighth note. Next, we have what we call as 32nd notes. These take half as much time as 16th notes, making them incredibly fast to play. However, the principle remains the same. Begin by picking the first note only while hammering on and pulling off the rest.

Once you are able to play the above at 80 bpm, turn the speed up a notch and continue practicing. Only move forward once you are able to execute the above without missing out or skipping a beat.

One Legato Coming Up

Let us start by using a simple C major scale. We will use three notes per string, formed as triplets, and will start ascending using hammer ons, and then descend using pull offs. Try and ensure that you use the right pressure when striking the note with your finger or pulling the already pressed fret, otherwise you may not get much of a result.

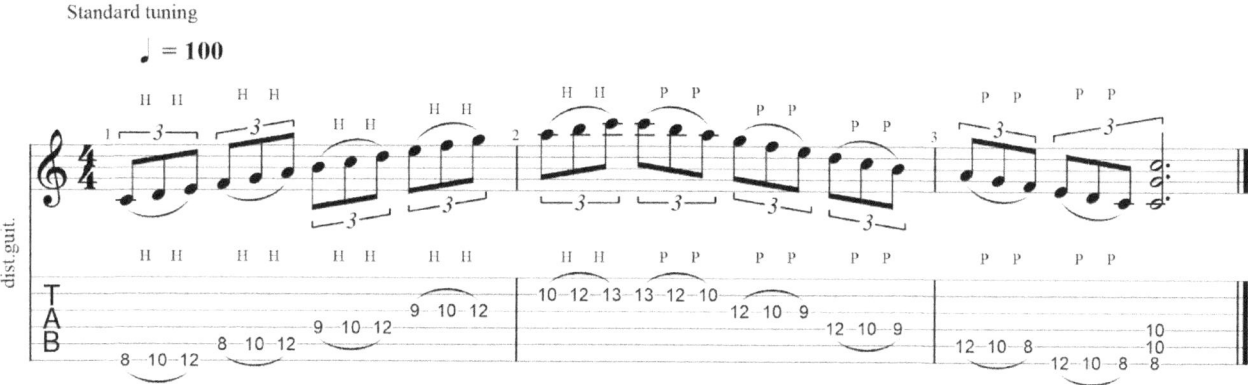

This one was fairly easy, right? It involved a series of 'Hs' followed by 'Ps' but this next one is a bit different. See if you can try to execute this one as smoothly as you did the last one.

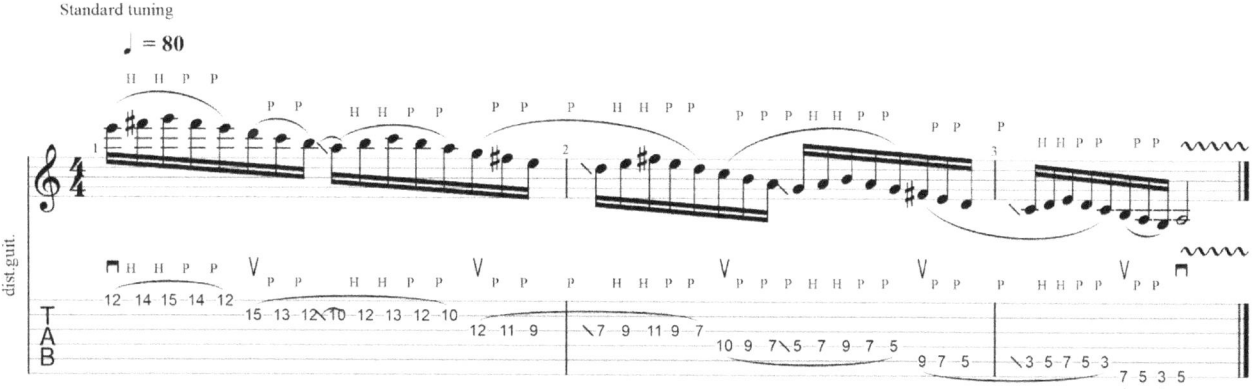

This one uses G major, and should pose some challenges, and if it does, it is perfectly normal. There is no need to be intimidated by the fact that there are so many notes and such little time. Practice with lower tempo settings and gradually increase your speed. Pay special attention to moments where you will need to change the string you are working on. Get that wrong and you risk missing a note completely, and that can throw your bandmates out of synchronization.

Speaking of synchronization, not all notes fall in a sequence. There are times where you may need to improvise a little, just to add that extra punch to the song or part of the song, and that is where you will need to rearrange the order of the scale. To help you with that, here are two examples of how such a lick would look like.

The above uses the G Major scale in the key of G. What's different about this one is the fact that you do not get a clean pass through. You have to maneuver your skills by picking up some notes and applying legato to some. Furthermore, I have deliberately changed the order of the scale, meaning that instead of the usual "1 2 4" approach, I have shuffled things around. This isn't to make your life difficult at all, but it is to train you to make these movements and adjustments more fluently when your playing really matters.

Practice around by picking up any scale of your choosing and rearranging the order, without overriding the scale notes or pattern. Use legato in combination with the traditional picking, or alternate pick, where possible. You can throw in vibrato to further highlight the notes and make them more expressive.

Here is one that is played in the style of **Tim Miller**, the iconic guitarist known for his supreme legato licks and hybrid picking. This is tough, but give it a whirl, and enjoy the sweet sounds you come across.

> **SIDE-NOTE:** *The 'T' you see is a tap. Don't worry if you are unable to play that as we will discuss that in a later chapter.*

As mentioned, this one is a bit tougher than your normal licks, and uses C#/Db blues scale. These are played as 'quintuples' or series of five notes. Don't worry much about that jargon and instead focus on executing these nicely.

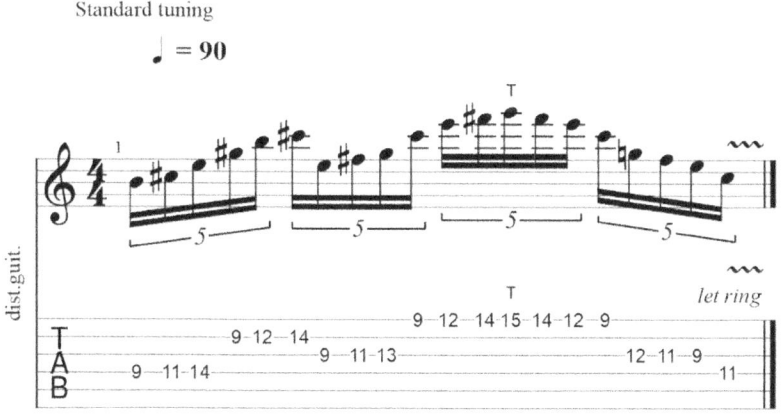

To further excel your legato skills, here are a few more licks to try out.

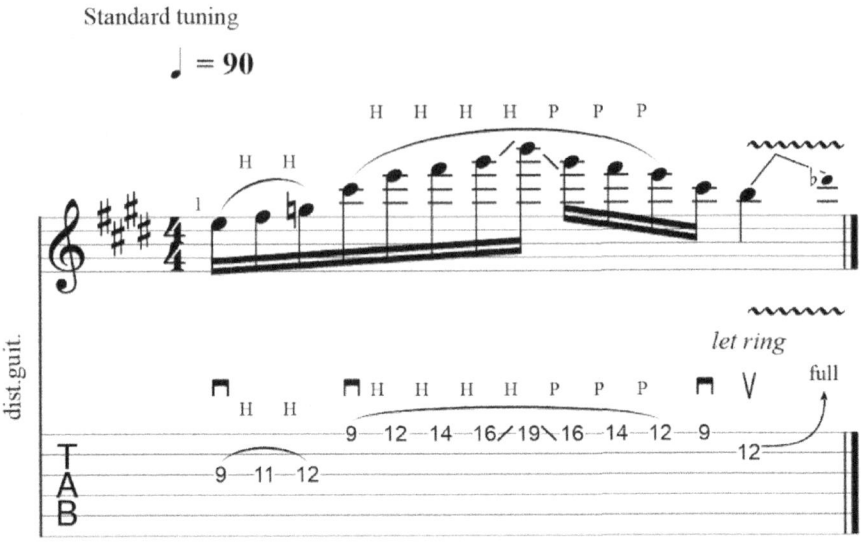

Next, we have two licks inspired by the legato techniques of none other than **Joe Satriani**. These can be intimidating, but they are well worth the perseverance and efforts.

American guitarist Joe Satriani performs during a concert in Shanghai, China, 14 February 2017. © ChinaImages

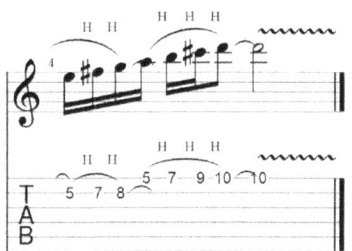

(D major)

And another one!

(D Major)

And finally, two more licks using sextuplets (six notes). These are equally fun to play, and certainly do pose a bit of challenge as well. Remember, focus on your hammer-ons and pull-offs, and the speed would come to you naturally.

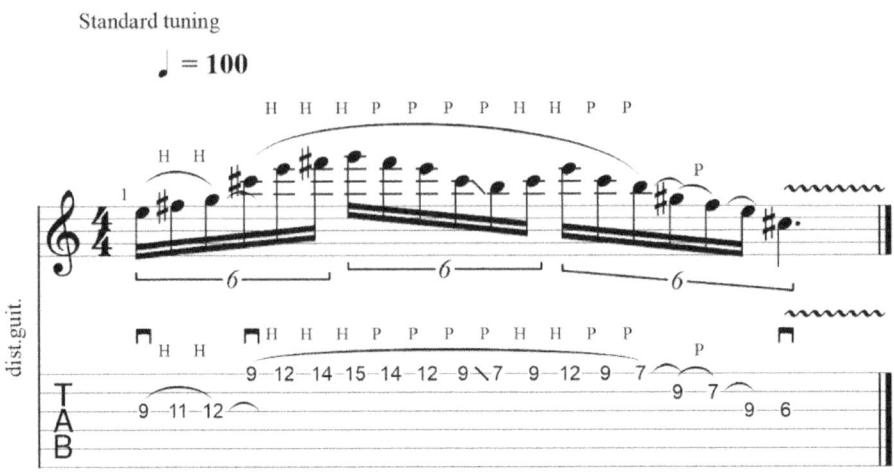

(C#)

The above takes a lot of practice. The tempo is quite fast, and the sixteenth note isn't exactly the most friendliest at times. Give it time, and your speed and accuracy should develop well with time.

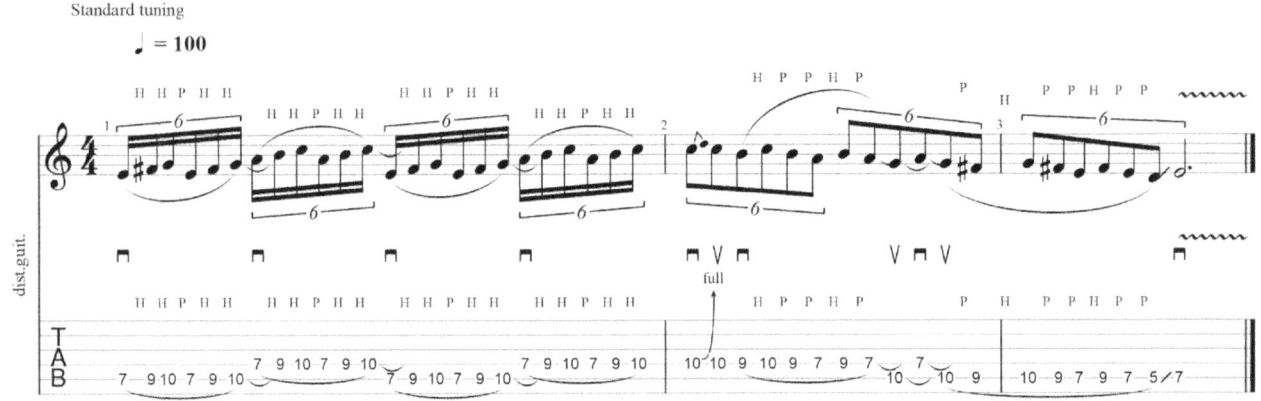

(G major)

Hopefully, you were able to tag along and found the above exercises fun and informative. All of the licks you have come across so far, and all those that you will, can be modified, altered, and used with any scale or key. Just do the necessary shifting and the rest is just smooth sailings.

Now that legato is out of the way, it is time to focus on my all-time favorite technique of bending. Yes, there is a lot more than just bending a string up or down, and these little details can help you pack in a lot more quality to your songs than you might think possible.

CHAPTER 5:

Bending

It is safe to say that every guitarist, irrespective of their genre or style of playing, uses the bending technique. Whether it is a semitone, or a whole tone, or even something called pre-bend, guitarists all around the world love and adore this technique as it greatly enhances the connection between two notes and adds a human touch to it. Otherwise, everything would sound robotic and monotonous.

Bending can also be incorporated with vibrato, to further add expressions. It is something that guitarists use and rely on heavily. As for who goes on to use this technique, a few names pop up immediately. These names include:

- Jimi Hendrix
- BB King
- Carlos Santana
- Stevie Ray Vaughn
- Eric Clapton
- Brian May

Since some of these are considered as godfathers of the rock and roll era, it is safe to assume that whatever they did, it worked. While each of them will be remembered in history for their contribution to music, all of them used the bend technique without compromise, which further cements the importance of this technique.

With that said, let's dive in and get started.

Bending the String Right

Just as the name suggests, the technique involves bending the string up or down. However, how you bend it, how far the bend goes, all of that matters quite a lot.

To begin with, there are four types of bending techniques in existence, and while many continue to use all of them, it is okay if you prefer to use one or two of these. As long as the concept is clear, and you have a firm command on your bending skills, the results should speak for themselves.

The four types of bends are:
- Semitone bend
- Whole tone bend
- Bend and release
- Pre-bend

Let us look at each of these to better understand how they work, and then try to incorporate these into our skillset.

Semitone Bend

We know that a note, when played in its natural position, it creates a specific sound or a musical note. We also know that if we were to go one fret higher, we would move half-step up, or one semitone up. Using the same principle, if we were to bend the string halfway up or down, we would change the note by one semitone.

Suppose, if you are to play the note 'A' on any given string, and then bend the string up as the note continues to ring, it will change its tone by half-a-step. As that happens, you will be able to hear the pitch of the note change by a semitone and then producing the note 'A#' as a result. This is how the semitone bend principle works.

To bend a note, you will first need to play the note in its natural place. Once it is attacked by the pick, and the note rings, only then can you execute a semitone bend to create another note without actually changing the fret position. This is something guitarists commonly do, especially towards the end of the scale position, or if they just wish to add in the next semitone into their lick.

Here is how a semitone bend would look like in standard notation and tabs.

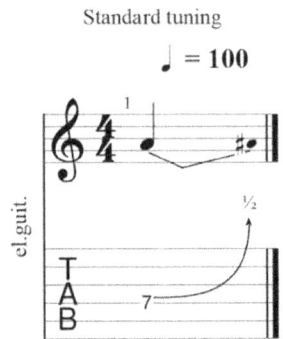

When a note is to be bent, it will always indicate whether the bend must be a semitone or a whole tone. For semitone, you will see the angular lines starting from the original note and leading to the note that is played as a result of the pull. In this case, A is being bent to produce the sound of A#. In tabs form, you will see the "½" symbol right above the arrow.

While the arrow may point upwards in the tab form, know that you can always go the other way and bend as well. This is just a representation of how tabs work and how bend is reflected on tabs.

With that said, play the above note and then execute a bend so that the note, as it is playing, changes the sound from A to A#. You can use a tuner to help you understand if you are able to execute a proper bend, and that the correct note is played.

The lick below is meant to help you practice the semitone bend. Give it a go and see how it sounds.

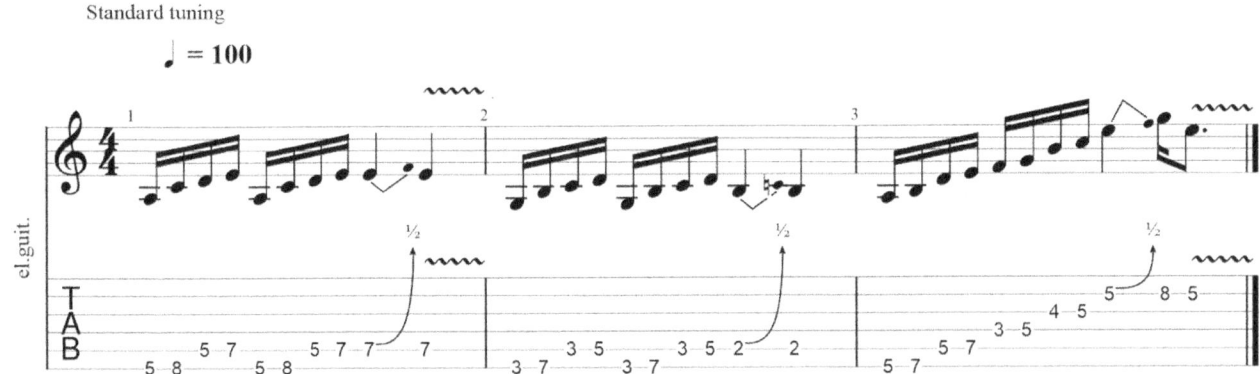

Whole Tone Bend

Whole tone bend, or full note bend, is just double the semitone bend. Where the first one goes halfway through, this one takes another half step, hence changing one complete tone, or going ahead one whole step from the actual note.

This one is represented by the word "full" on tabs and a similar looking angular line in the standard notations, with just a minor difference of the angle's height. It can often be confusing, which is why I recommend you study music using both the notations and the tabs.

For the whole bend technique, here is a great exercise. It is small, but it is fun to play and allows you to use multiple bends in a period of two bars only.

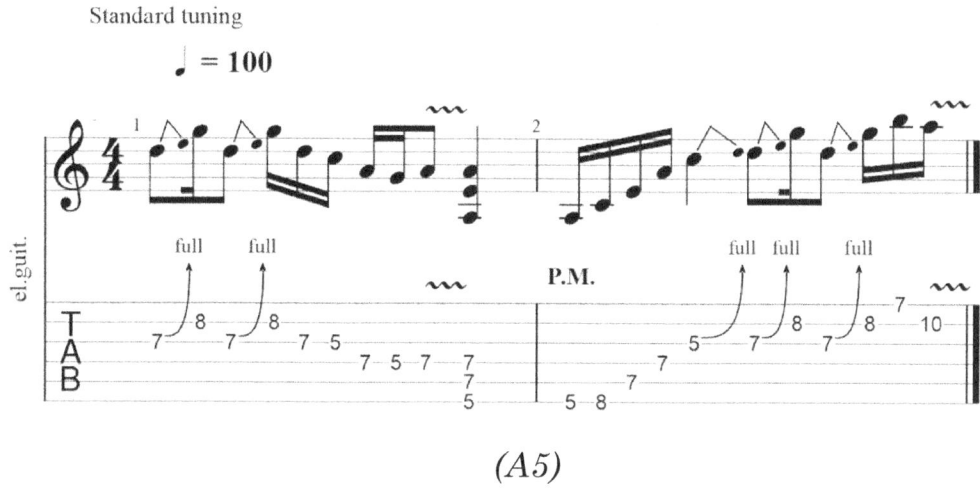

(A5)

Bend and Release

Bend is released is exactly how it sounds. You bend the string, play the note, and while the bent note is played, you start releasing the string until it comes back to its original place. The action of doing so allows you to get a note that went up and then comes back down.

The bend and release is represented using two curvy arrow signs. One goes and the other immediately follows in a drop. If you played the lick above, here is a modified version of the same lick. All the notes are exactly the same, but I have only changed the bending technique here. You will notice that this sounds a lot more interesting, or at least different from the one you played earlier.

Even though the above is played with the same A5 progression, it does sound different, doesn't it? Well, now you can change your favorite solo and make it a little more interesting than it already was. If, by any chance, you were already using this technique, well done you!

Pre-Bend

Pre-bend sounds simple in theory, but the practical application can often be a bit tricky. If you are someone like me, and you are also a big fan of **Slash**, you might have heard his famous Godfather solo that he performed in a concert in Japan. In that specific solo, he has used almost every bending technique in the book, including the pre-bend.

The pre-bend technique is essentially a way to bend the string first and then strike the note.

"Why not just use the next fret instead?"

It does make sense to use the actual fret position instead, but that would be running ahead of ourselves. The pre-bend allows you to do something no other technique can get done. It can allow you to bend in the opposite way. Generally, you bend a string and it goes a semitone or a full note ahead. With the pre-bend, you are already there, and as you release it, it goes backwards. Unlike the bend and release, where we play the original note before bending, here the original note is one that is already bent up when played. The result would be a silky smooth transition to a lower note, leaving many to wonder "How on earth did he do that?"

The pre-bend is shown in multiple ways, as shown in the lick below.

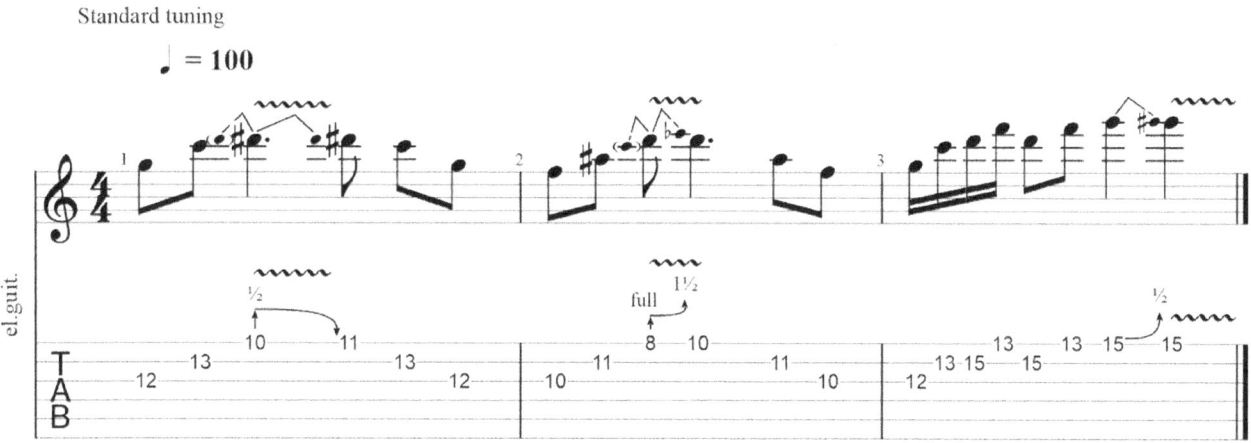

In the first bar (D#maj13), the 10th fret position on the first string is pre-bent by one semitone, and once its played, it is released, creating a smooth transition from 11th note to the 10th note. Next, in the second bar (Dm7#5) we have something called Pre-bend and Bend. You pre-bend the string by one whole note, play the pre-bent note, and then bend the string further by half a step. Be careful as I would not recommend doing this technique on strings which are either detuned or far too stiff as this can easily cause strings to snap. The final bar uses Dm11.

Let us now combine all the four techniques and test our skills.

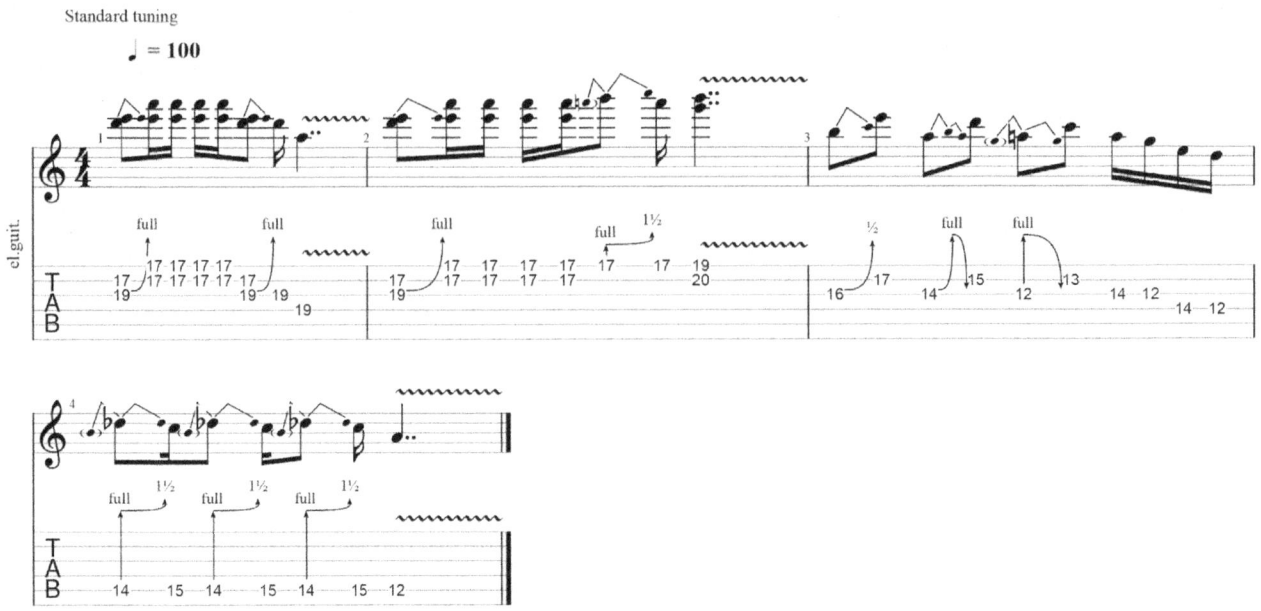

For the blues fan, here's one that would certainly give you some good vibes.

(D9add(7))

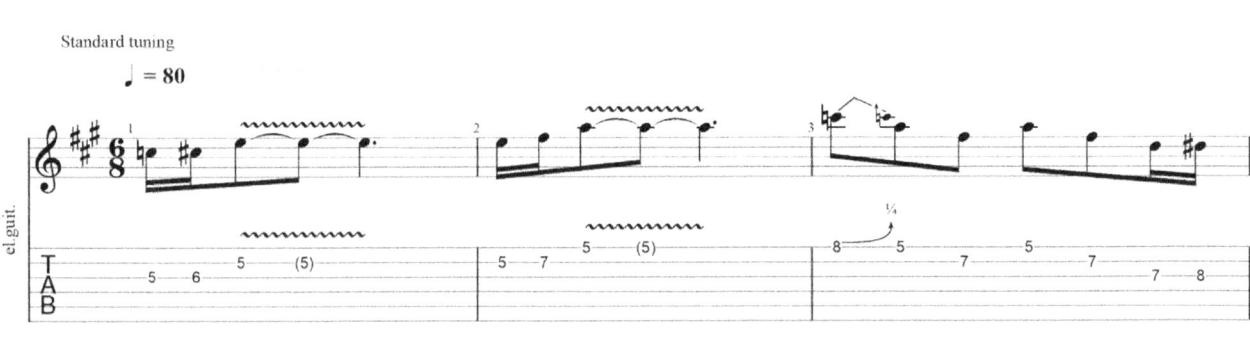

Get ready to tire your fingers out with the next lick.

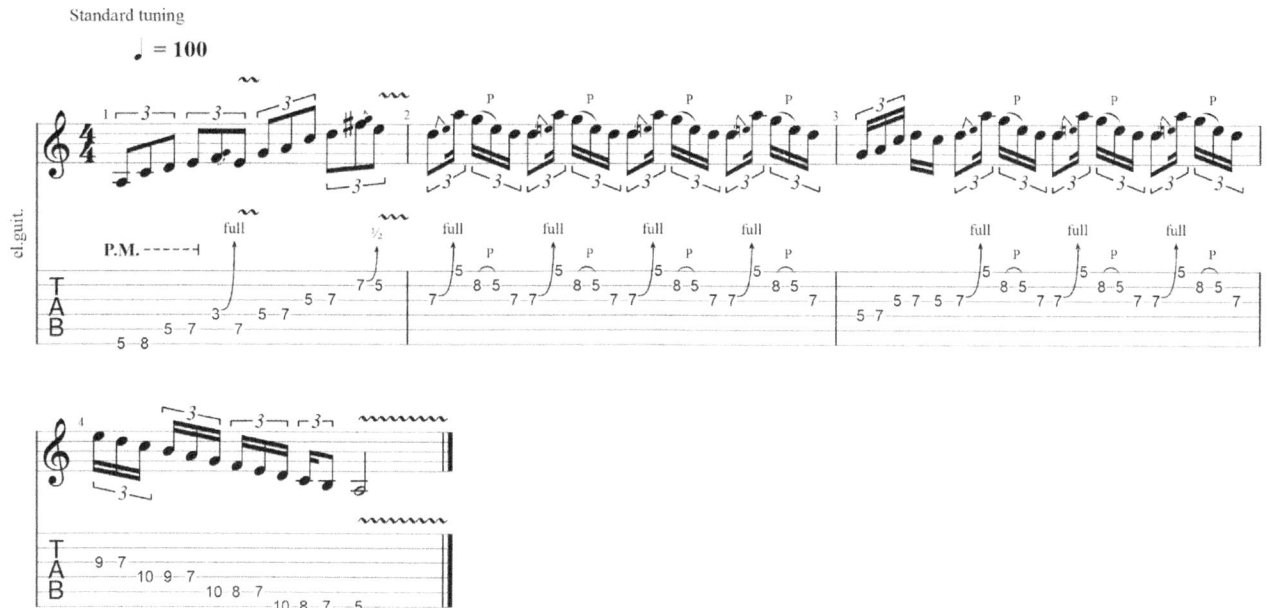

You would normally encounter such licks in many genres, including blues, rock, metal and more. These are often used repeatedly to create a fantastic fill, and still keep the momentum going. However, as incredible as they sound, they are equally challenging to master. Do not rush through this one until you are 100% sure that you can pull this off without looking at the fretboard.

Licks Worth Knowing

Since I mentioned all the great legends who use the bending technique, let us use them as inspiration and practice on licks which can help us learn how to play like them. Each of these licks are inspired by these great guitarists, and they are not taken from any of their songs. If you are interested to learn their songs instead, you can search the internet, but be warned that there would not be a learning curve involved in mimicking someone else. With that said, let's dig in!

BB King style

Since it is **BB King** style, all three licks are using the key of B. It is also to be noticed that BB Kings really loved to mix minor and major pentatonic scales together, as shown under, so expect some twist.

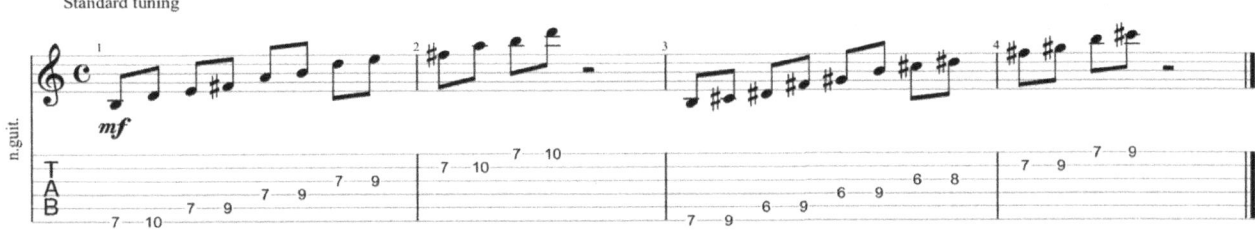

Lick 1

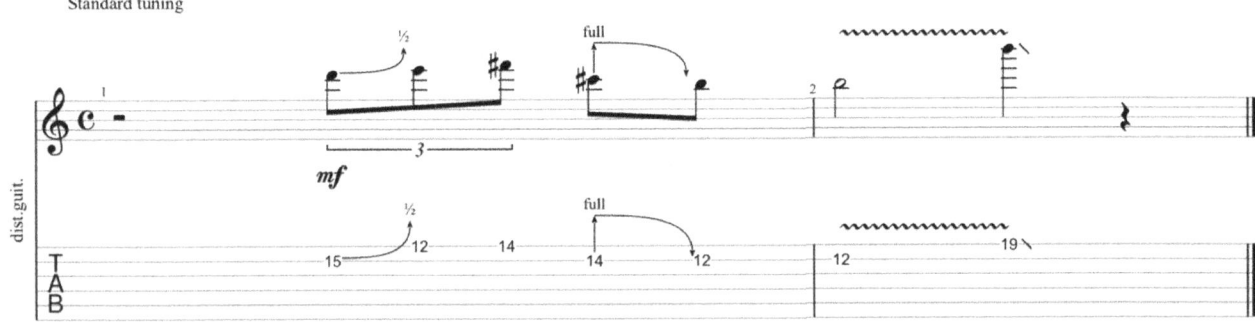

Lick 2

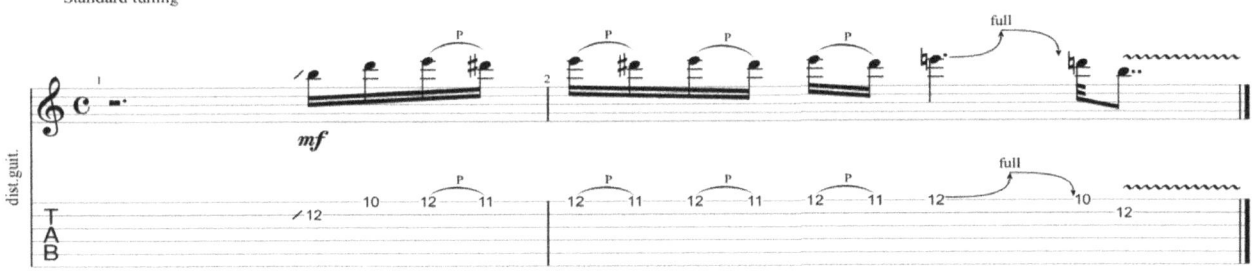

Lick 3

Eric Clapton

The following two licks are pretty standard, and **Clapton** has used these with variations. Once you get the hang of these, you should have no problem modifying or even adopting other variations by Clapton himself.

Lick 1 (A5)

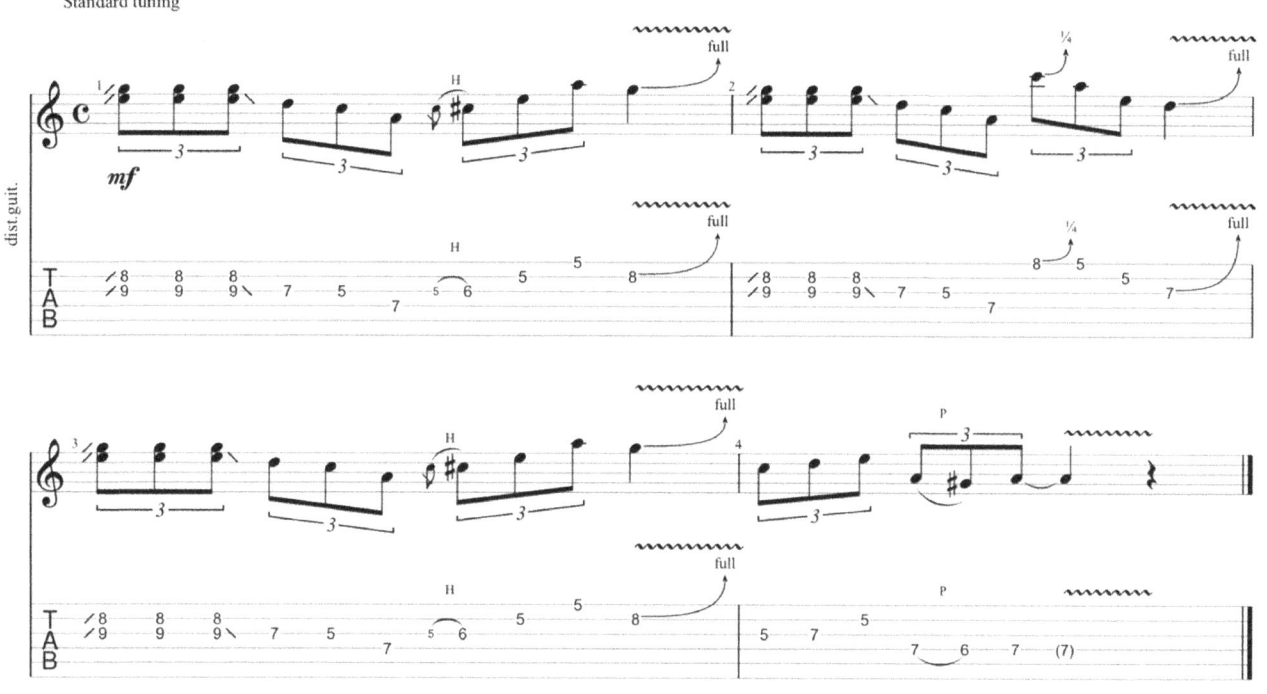

Lick 2 (A7 leading to E7)

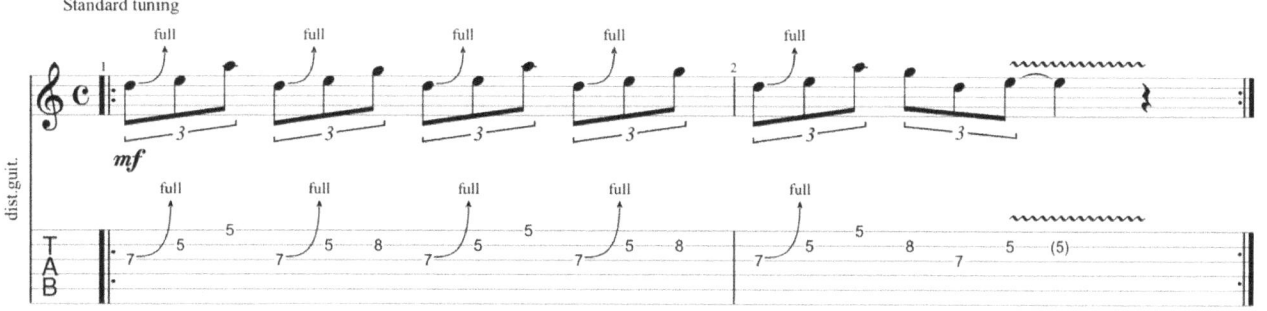

Stevie Ray Vaughan

His licks were never too simple. The licks you are about to see use the **key of E**, and sometimes he used to tune his guitar half-step down, further adding to the charm. These are slightly different, but still well worth the efforts.

Lick 1

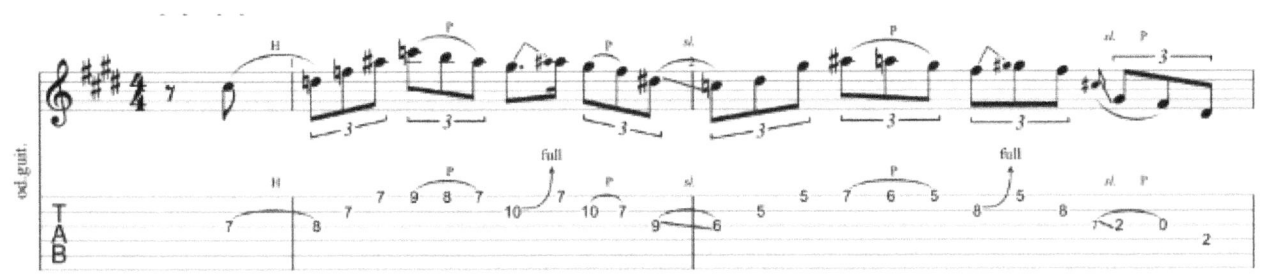

Lick 2

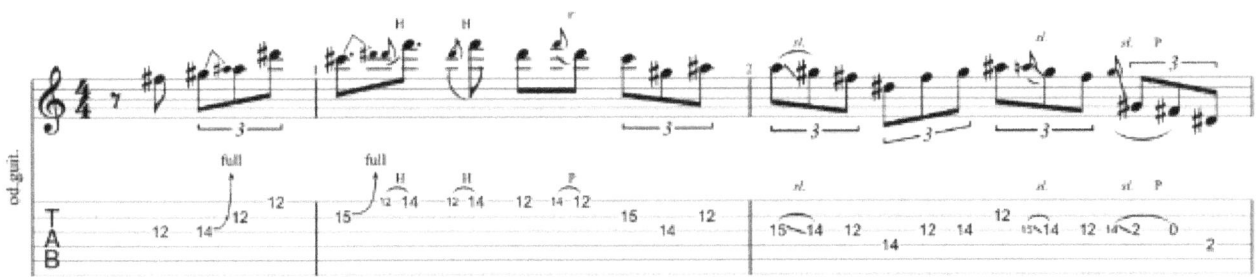

Of course, coming in the style of the legend himself, his licks are often complicated, but they are the stuff of every guitarist's wild dreams. Play any of these before moving into the song, or before beginning your solo, and the audience would be begging you to play more.

Jimi Hendrix

For those who may not know who **Jimi Hendrix** is, let me give you a quick introduction. He is considered as the godfather of the rock and roll era. A guitarist who redefined playing, introduced the world to creativity that was never heard of, seen or experienced by any. He died at the age of 27, but he left behind a legacy that is still remembered today.

His work needs no introduction to guitarists, especially those who are fond of using licks with bending techniques. Despite the young age, he went on to influence the world and allowed many other legendary guitarists to take a leaf from his knowledge and prowess.

Below, you will see two of my most favorite licks, played in the style of Jimi Hendrix. The first lick uses **E7, G and A chords**.

Lick 1

Lick 2

This one is longer, and a bit more complicated. However, do not let that intimidate you. Try and work as much as you can to understand how this masterpiece works. You would be amazed how simple **E, A and G chords** can be used to create something this astonishing.

The above uses something called 'Trill' and that is essentially using only the notes indicated for the rest of the bar by hammer on and pull off only. The rest is relatively easy as the pace of the song is moderate, allowing beginners to take full advantage of the moment and learn something that would go on to benefit their musical journeys, especially in the arena of blues.

Carlos Santana

Yet another name that many have overlooked in recent years. **Carlos Santana** set the tone and proved to the world just why he is worthy of being a legend. His creative approach, his stylish techniques, and his facial and musical expressions are a sight worth seeing and experiencing.

Carlos Santana
© ndenisov

Writing down licks in his style was a mammoth task, but not one that is impossible. Using the **Am7 and D7 chords**, with a hint of a twist, here is the first lick that you should familiarize yourself with.

Lick 1

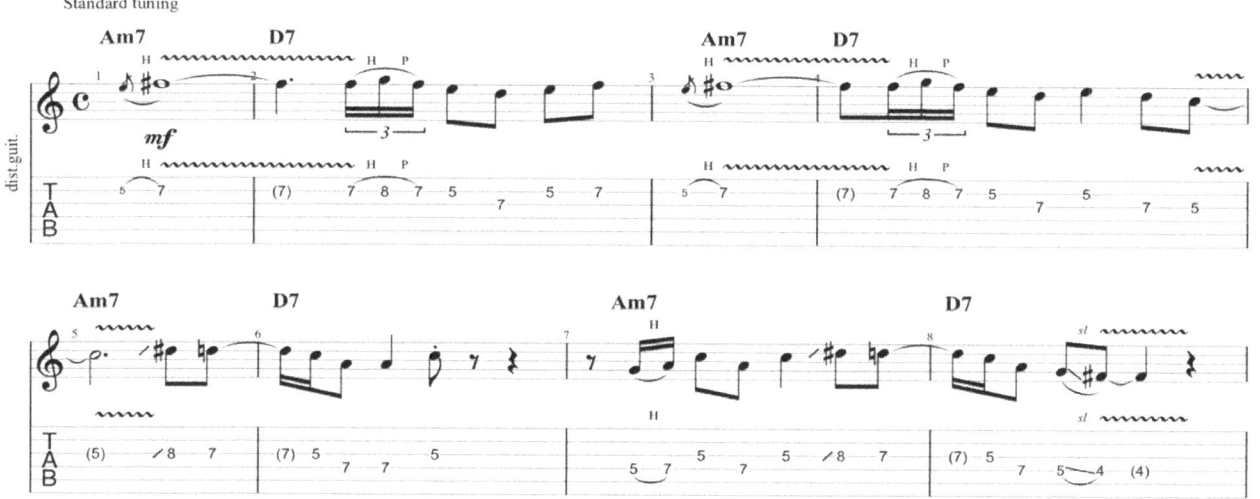

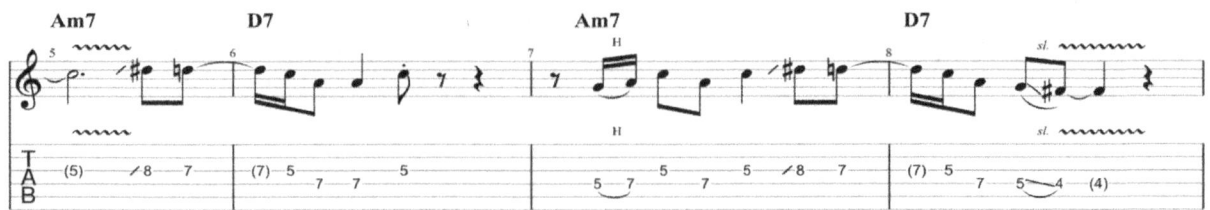

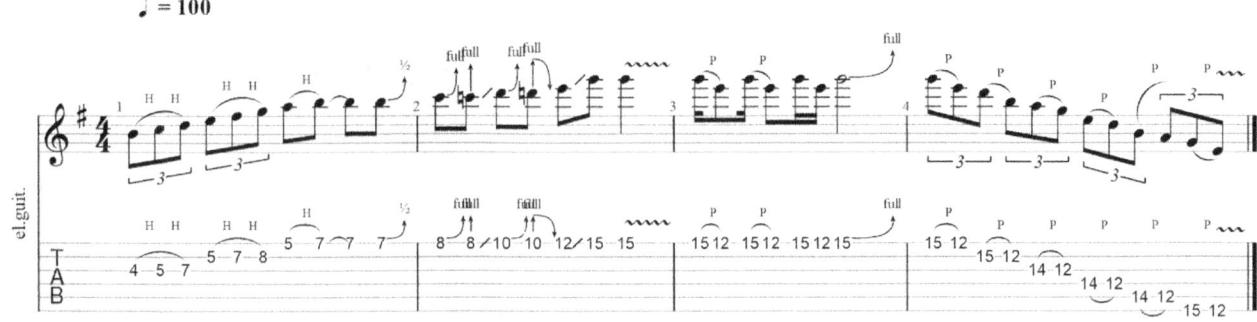

Lick 2 (Key of E minor)

All the bends used are full, whether whole note bend or pre-bends. Since they are too closely knitted together, I thought it would be a good idea to clarify that right away.

Well, hopefully the licks I provided above have helped you in improving your bending techniques, and also given you a fair idea of how powerful bending is. It is time now for us to move forward to the next chapter where we will learn about something called the economy picking. Learn this, and I promise that your friends would be dying to learn how you do that.

CHAPTER 6:

Economy Picking — You May Know It as Sweep Picking

Sweep picking is one of the sweetest ways to impress your friends, astonish and amaze the onlookers and pull off some incredibly fast licks, with the least amount of efforts. Yes, it is possible.

The technique of sweep picking has been around ever since the invention of the plectrum (pick) itself (Griffiths, 2020) . Many great guitarists of our time and even before us continued to use this technique to play a variety of notes in quick succession. It is easy to see why people often consider this as a shredding technique, and it has everything to do with the way it is executed.

Some famous names who used, or use, the economy picking technique include:

- Frank Gambale
- George Benson
- Jason Becker
- Steve Vai
- Yngwie Malmsteen

I mentioned Malmsteen in the end because it is him who single-handedly redefined the use of the technique through his approach. He alone inspired at least two generations of guitarists, and gave the world one monumental technique to learn and use.

The Technique

The concept of sweep picking is to use your pick and sweep it through the strings in one fluid motion, and as you do so, you continue to change notes on that corresponding string. This swift motion can often be as quick as a blink of an eye, and that means that within a fraction of a second, the guitarist would execute numerous notes from top to bottom, and probably make his way back as well.

To show just how this is done, here are a few exercises I have lined up for you. For ascending motions, use the downstroke on all strings. For descending motions, use the upstroke of the pick for each string that is played. Take it as a strum, which you would normally do when playing a chord. However, instead of playing them all at the same time, you play each note individually with the same speed. It is hard, but it is not impossible.

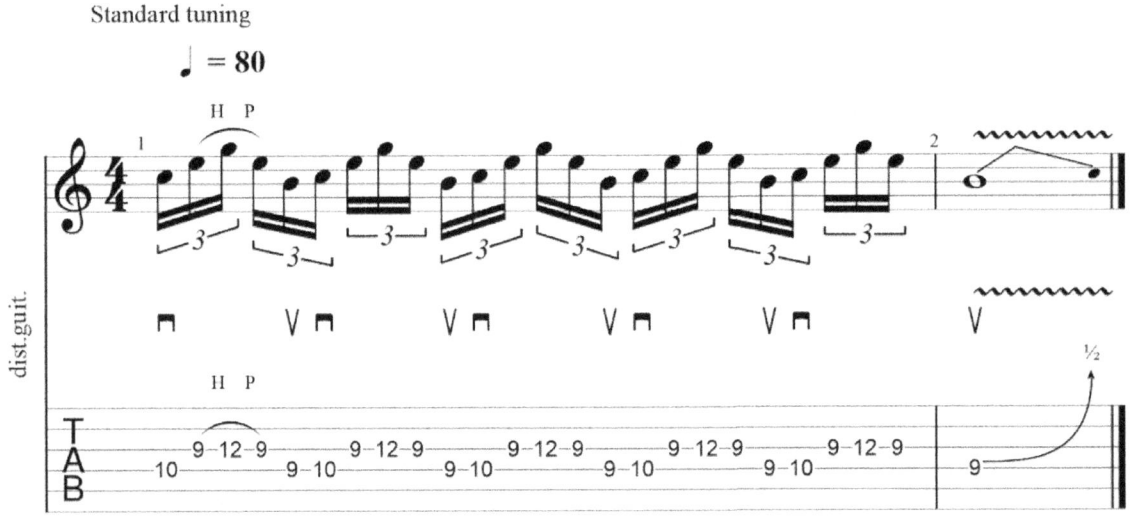

The above uses a Cmaj7 chord and gives you a rough idea of what sweep picking is like. It is certainly a lot like legato, but where legato can incorporate both downstroke and upstroke at the same time, here the downstroke is only done when the guitarist wishes to ascend. For the opposite direction, you already know what they need to do.

Here is another lick, this time using the Dmaj7/C#.

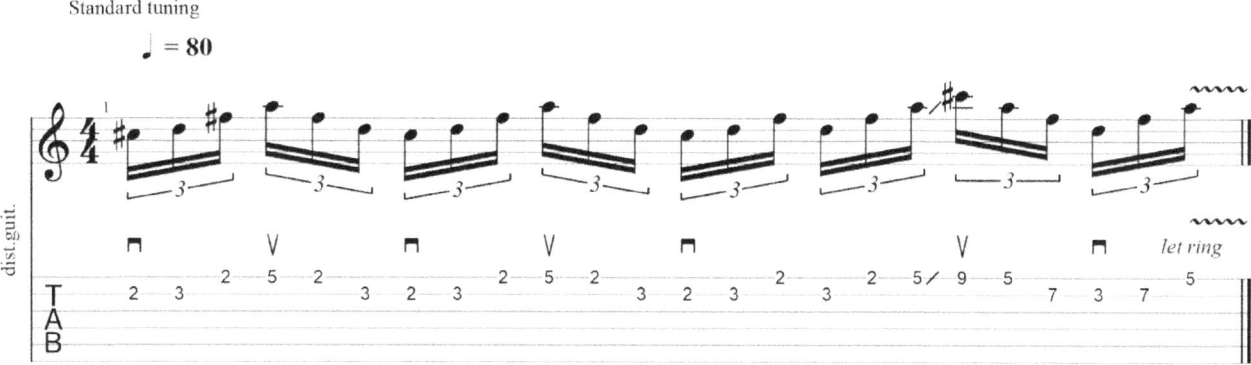

For our avid readers, you may have already spotted that I am using arpeggios, and there is a good reason for that. Arpeggios are a perfect way to get started and practice your skills with. They may be awfully close to scales, but they are indeed a separate thing. They are more melodic, and they can be used in a variety of ways.

Why Do Guitarists Use Sweep Picking?

It is a good question, and one that I actually had back in the day when I was learning how to play guitars.

If you were to play any of the above licks with alternate picking, you would soon be struggling to maintain the rhythm and the flow of the notes. That happens because you will be moving your hand or wrist up in an up and down motion far too many times. It would eventually cause you to be exhausted, burned out, and you may even have to sleep the night with a wrist that feels like it's broken (Ouch!).

Sweep picking, on the other hand, helps you to do the same hard work without the actual hard work. You still get to play the licks just as you please, and get to use your picking hand just a fraction of what you would otherwise be using. Your pick hand is at ease, and your left hand can take things up a notch and increase the speed as well. You will no longer be dependent on how fast your picking hand can manage.

For the next four exercises, I will be using two strings and three strings sweep picking licks. Once you have learned how to execute those, we can then move on to the real deal.

"What do you mean by that?"

Well, if you were under the impression that sweep picking is only done with two or three strings, you're in for a big surprise.

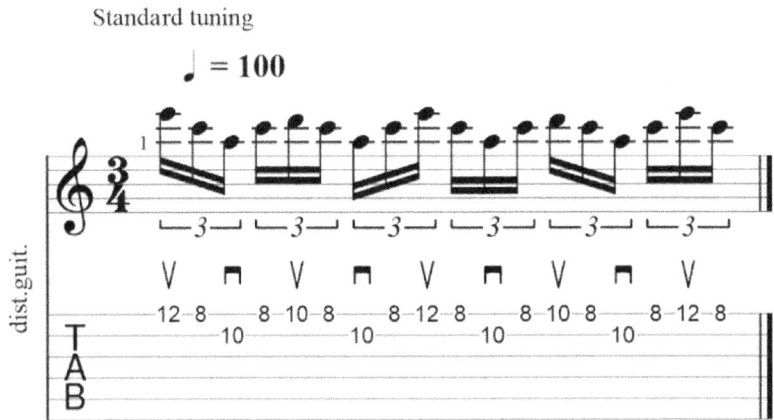

Now, we will use the first three strings to pull off a seemingly simple but beautiful arpeggio. The following uses the G Minor chord. Pay special attention to the way the downstroke works. The objective is to allow the pick to glide through the strings in one swift downward motion. As it goes down, it will attack the next string and that's where you'd already be in position to play the note.

See how we are only using the pick seldomly? This is the beauty of sweep picking. It gets the job done, without making you feel tired, exhausted, or even finding yourself at risk of desynchronizing with your left hand. It is a worthy trait, and all the major guitarists using this technique only cements its dominance, use, significance and quality.

I have deliberately created a longer lick for you where you will start from a quarter note. Two bars later, you will switch to eighth notes, sixteenth and finally triplets sixteenth notes. The focus here should be on how you switch your downstroke to upstroke and vice versa. Let it be as natural as possible, and glide as smoothly as you can. You will be stunned at how you will find yourself playing faster and faster than ever before.

Here is one more three strings arpeggio, inspired and played in the style of **Malmsteen**. It uses the key of A minor, and has that perfect build up to

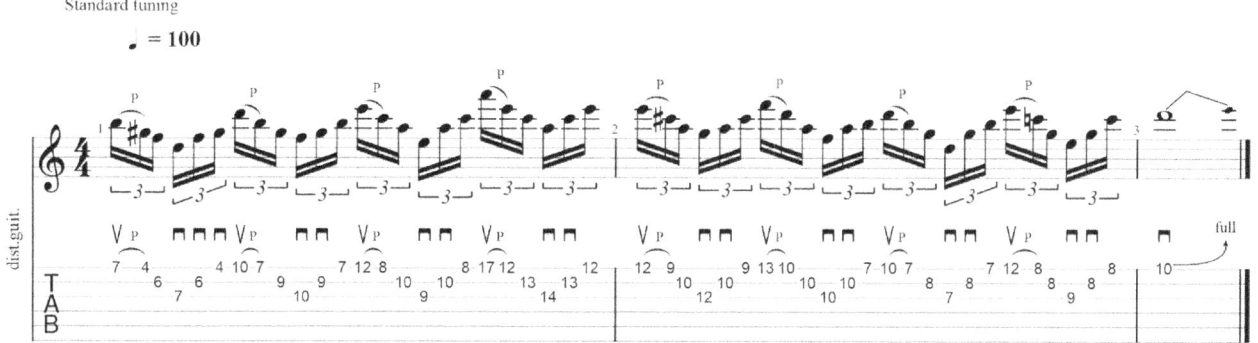

a solo or the start of a song that you may be about to play after this lick ends. Check it out yourself and see how it sounds.

Malmsteen sure knew how to introduce his solos and songs. His licks were perhaps the finest the world had ever seen, and to this day, there is no one who can match the calibre, the finesse and the sheer creativity Malmsteen brought to the table. This is the reason why many went on to be inspired by him, and used his techniques to become legends in their own rights.

Adding Another String

Like I said earlier, sweep picking continues to grow more impressive of a technique, and at the same time, it can get a lot more intimidating as well. What you are about to witness and experience now is a four strings sweep pick lick, or two. Once you have found your rhythm with the earlier ones, these should actually be a lot more fun to perform and play.

The following two use the keys of Fm, Cm, Gm, Dm and Em. I have broken them down into two parts so that I could first encourage you to learn each of these two. Once you have mastered them, combine both of them together for an even more melodical venture.

Lick 1

Lick 2

It is worth noting that sweep picking isn't your everyday alternate picking exercise. This can take time, and by that I mean weeks or even months to master. Do not rush nor pace through the process of learning. Let the learning take its course, and continue to practice. Along the way, you will encounter challenges, such as missing beats or playing the wrong note, but with time you will start getting the hang of things.

Mastering Sweep Picking

Below, you will find some exquisite licks to practice and master. All of these will use sweep picking and some other techniques which we have already encountered before.

Lick 1 (Ionian ascending and Dorian descending)

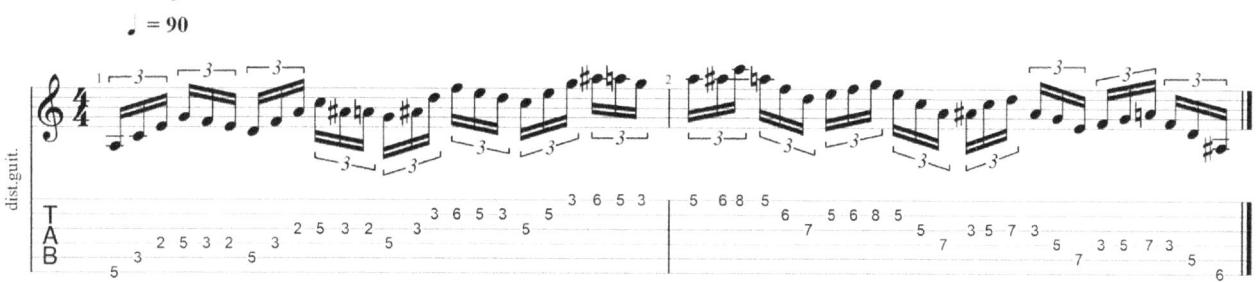

Lick 2 (Dm7, G7, C7)

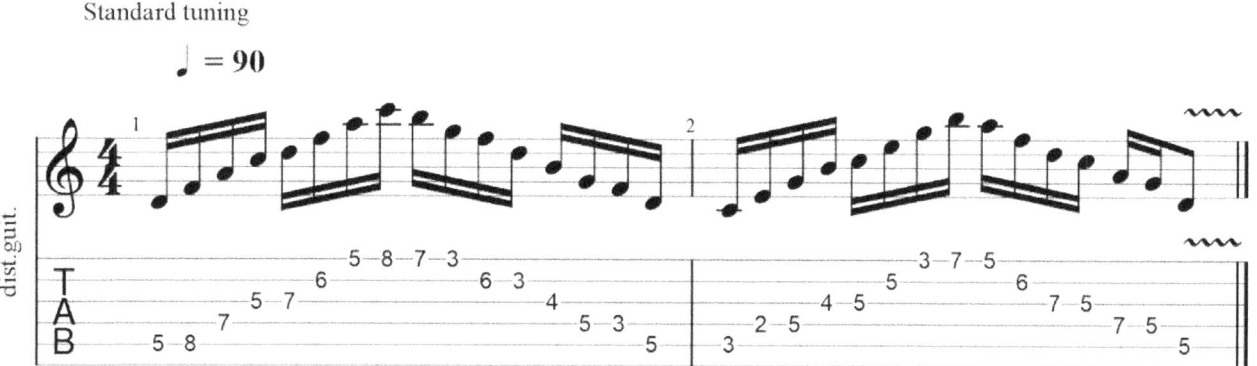

Lick 3 (Seven chord progression, key of A)

Lick 4 (Gmaj7, F#m7)

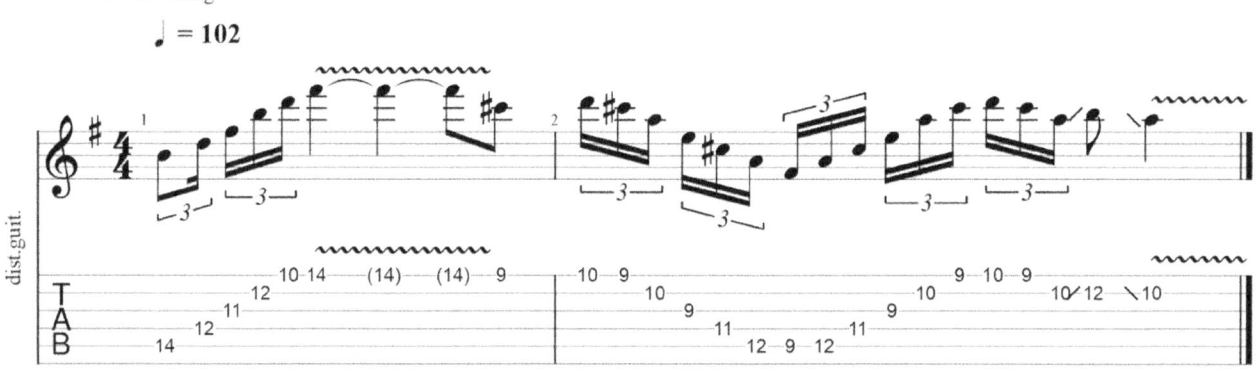

Lick 5 (Bb, C)

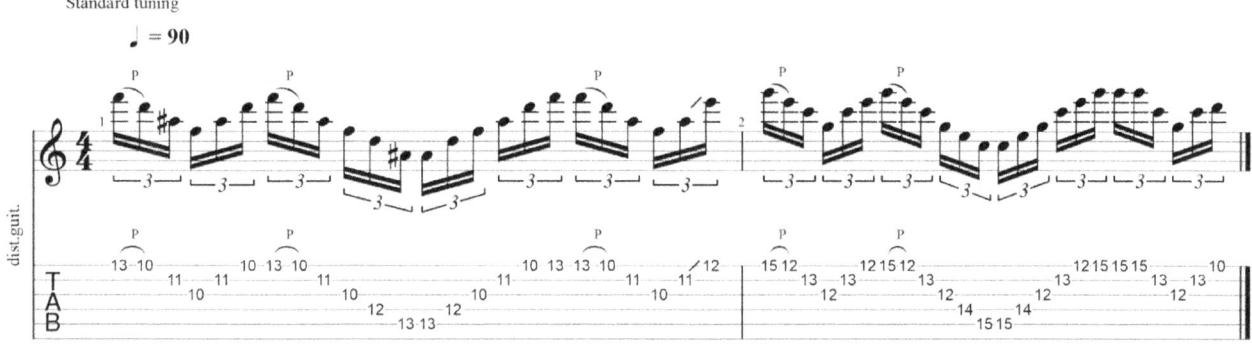

Lick 6 (In style of Frank Gambale — Amin7)

Lick 7 (In style of Frank Gambale — Dmin7)

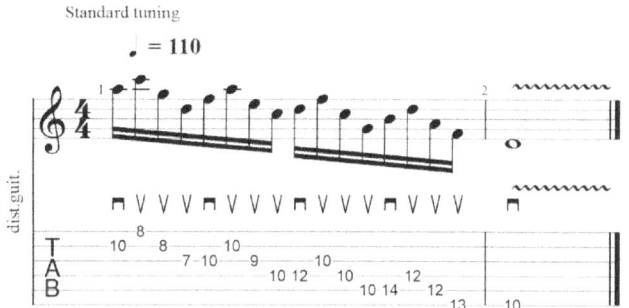

Philippe Frenette-Roy, CC BY-SA 3.0 <https://creativecommons.org/licenses/by-sa/3.0>, via Wikimedia Commons

This one may be simpler, as compared to many others, but the major reason for that is the fact that I have used a slower tempo (110 bpm). Once you have enough practice, use higher bpm, such as 160, to fully harness the magnificent results.

Lick 8 (A minor neoclassical)

Well, hopefully the above should leave you with a lot of creative ideas, and loads of practice sessions. Once again, the key here is to ensure smoothness and execution of the technique and notes, not the speed. The speed, I assure you, will come to you with practice.

With that said, it is now time to bid farewell to the sweep picking and head on to another advanced technique called hybrid picking. If sweep picking was a delight, the next technique will be the cherry on the top.

CHAPTER 7:

Hybrid Picking — Using Pick and Fingers

I assure you that this is not something out of a science-fiction book. This technique is very real, and it is one of the finest ways to play multiple strings at the same time.

While this type of picking has been around for sometime, it was in recent times that this technique gained an audience and attracted so much attention. The technique is revolutionary because it goes to assist the guitarist to essentially multi-task on the go.

The hybrid picking involves the use of your pick and your fingers, working in synchronization and each focusing on their respective strings. This means that if you have a lick which involves you to play the seventh fret on the D string, and you need to play ninth frets on both B and E strings at the exact same time, you can use this technique to get you out of a tough spot and deliver surprising results.

The technique is popular, but when it comes to who uses it the best, a few names do come to mind. These names would include:

- Albert Lee
- Gustavo Assis Brasil
- Brett Garsed

The technique may be new to you, but I am sure you have already visualized how this will work, and if you did that, well done!

The Era of Hybrid

Hybrid picking is easy to do. If you do not believe me, do the above example on your own and you will find out just how easy it can be applied to your own music.

There are a few advantages that the hybrid picking brings with itself. The most noticeable one is the fact that through hybrid picking, you can create more soothing sounds. While your pick creates a crisp note, your fingers would balance the crispness of the sound with the mellower and sweeter tones. Put these two together and you end up with music that soothes the soul and entices the artists out of you.

Make no mistake, this special type of picking is slightly more advanced than your usual alternate picking or other forms of picking. Considering that we are using both the pick and the fingers, all in perfect harmony, it is slightly more challenging.

Unlike any other technique that we have come across so far, this one requires you to use your fingers to pluck the notes, and that means that you will need the right fingernail length to ensure smooth experience. A little too long and you risk getting stuck playing the wrong string or getting in the way from one string to another. Get it too short, and you risk muting the string you are about to play. Ideally, you are looking to maintain one to two millimeters length for your nails.

Fingernail length is important, but what is even more important than that is the shape of your fingernail. If you have nails like I did once, which weren't exactly guitar-friendly, you will face quite a tough time.

The problem is that everyone has different curvature when it comes to nails. On top of that, there is no specific one-size-fits-all that I could tell you about. To find out what works for you, you will need to pick a strong slowly and focus on three important phases:

1. The contact point

2. The release point

3. String travel

Once you feel these three, you should be able to work out which nail shape works for you.

Now that we have that sorted, it is time to do a bit of hybrid picking.

The Technique

Let us begin by first understanding how we can read patterns and tablatures to understand which finger we need to use and when. Here is how a typical pattern would look like.

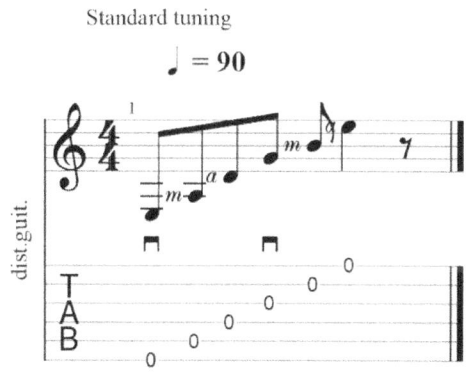

You begin with a downstroke on the sixth string. Then, you are to use your middle finger (*m*) to pick the next string, followed by your ring finger (*a*) for the next. Repeat the same for the last three strings.

What you essentially did there was hybrid picking. Sometimes, you will be required to do these separately, which is a lot easier, and then there will be moments where you may have to strike a note with your pick and pluck another string or two at the same time. That is where things can get a lot more confusing and tougher.

The Licks For the Job

Now that you have some basic idea of how hybrid picking works, or at least the easier way, let us look into some licks which are designed to teach you the practical aspects of hybrid picking. Remember, everything in this book takes practice. If you are not able to get it right the first few times, do not smash your guitar. It happens to the best of us, and take it from a guy who is anything but that. It took me ages before I was able to hone my skills and do hybrid picking.

Lick 1 (In style of Albert Lee — Uses E Major Key)

Foto: Andreas Lawen, Fotandi, CC BY-SA 4.0
<https://creativecommons.org/licenses/by-sa/4.0>,
via Wikimedia Commons

For the benefit of learning, you can use a slower tempo to begin your practice. There is no point in rushing through this.

Lick 2 — (In style of Albert Lee — Uses G Major key)

Once again, I have reduced the tempo. This is to ensure that anyone, who may be a beginner like I once was, has every chance to learn and not be intimidated by the lessons. For your convenience, I have only marked out the (m) and not the down or upstroke.

Lick 3 — (Pedal note exercise — Em, Am, B, Dm)

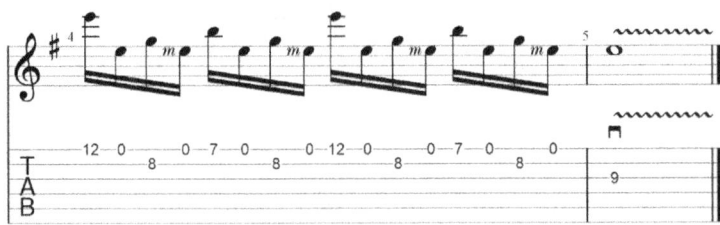

Lick 4 — (Pedal note exercise — E, A, B)

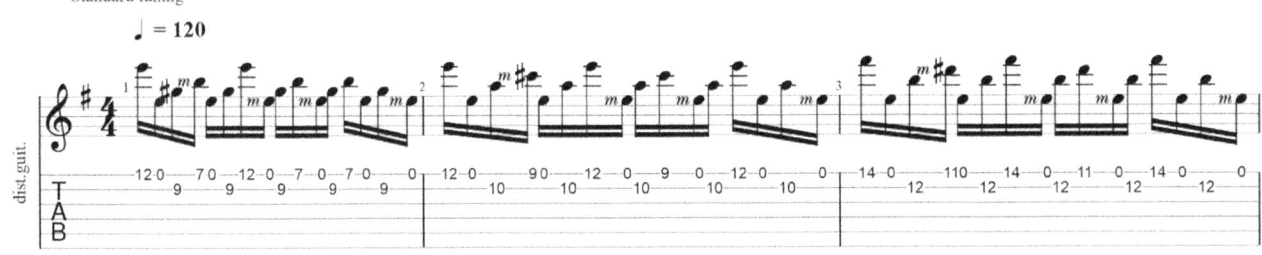

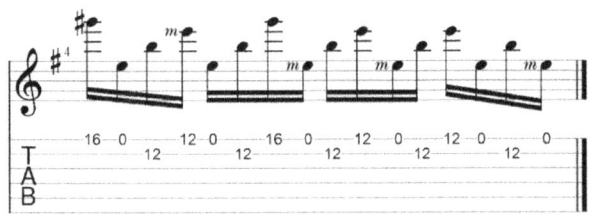

Lick 5 — (Arpeggiating with chords — Dsus2, Cadd9, G/B, D/A)

Lick 6 — (Arpeggiating — Em, Em9, Em6, Em(maj7), Em7)

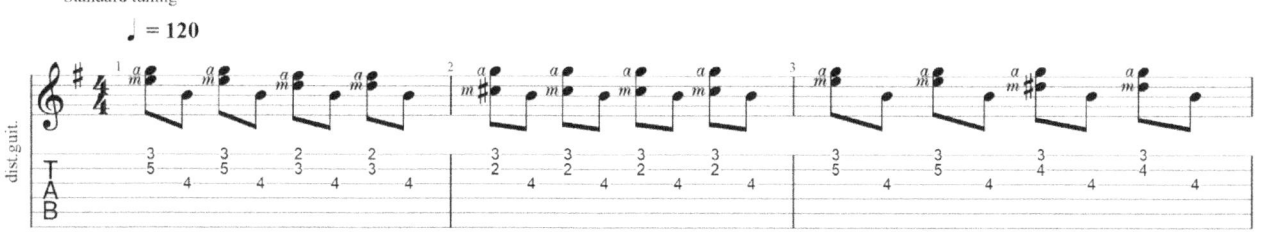

Lick 7 — (Banjo style licks)

Lick 8 — (banjo style)

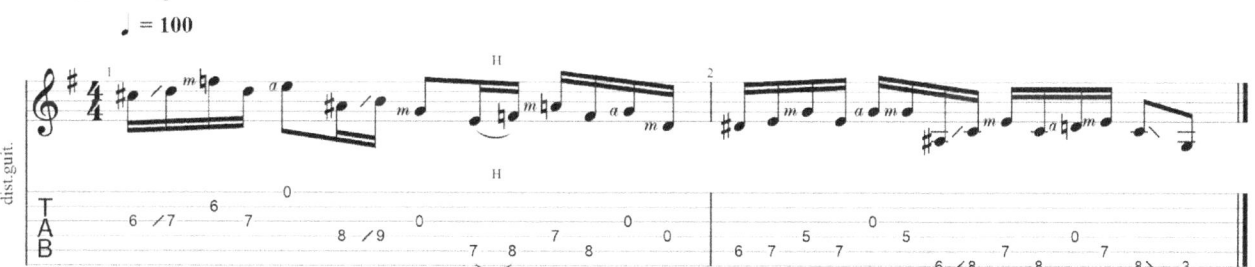

Lick 9 — (In style of Chet Atkins — A, D)

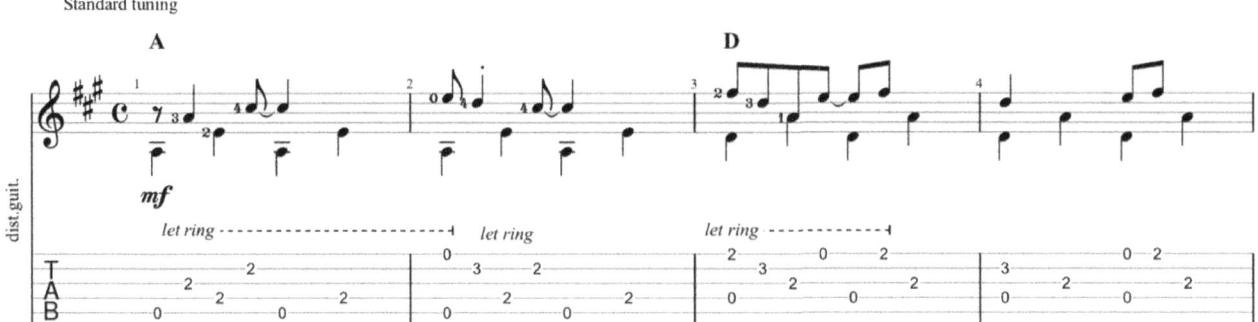

Jac. de Nijs / Anefo, CC0, via Wikimedia Commons

In the above, the purpose is to let the bass notes ring so that the fusion of other notes makes the entire experience more melodical.

Lick 10 — (In the style of Chet Atkins — D, E, E9, A)

Well, I do hope that this was yet another adventurous chapter, and that you now have something new to look forward to. It is not everyday that you wake up to find that you have a new skill to utilize as a guitarist. Take your time to absorb as much knowledge as you can, and take time to polish your skills.

In the next chapter, we will be looking at one of my favorite skills, tapping. Yes, we're there!

CHAPTER 8:

Tapping

Tapping has been made famous by many, many great artists around the world. It is one of those effortless yet extremely cool ways through which you can pull off a series of fast-paced notes, licks, and solos. Do it right and the world would be your audience.

If the above statement sounds "too unrealistic" or vague, have a look at these great names. They did exactly that, learned the art and defined an era for the rest of us guitarists to learn from:

1. Eddie Van Halen
2. Steve Vai
3. Reb Beach

Of course, I cannot go on talking about tapping without mentioning Van Halen. For those who may not know him, he is essentially the person who brought tapping on the map in the first place. However, we aren't here for a history lesson, which is why it is time to dig in and learn the trait ourselves.

Tap Your Notes Away

Let's begin by a simple exercise, to get your fingers warmed up. Tapping is essentially just as it sounds. You play a note somewhere, and then you either use your left hand (if playing an open string) or your right hand (to tap a note while the left hand holds the initial note). This is done in a fast paced manner, to ensure that the rhythm is not broken. However, before we jump into more technical tapping, let's start with a bit of **Satriani**. Using a pedal note (one that you play continuously), we will use our left hand to do the tapping (marked with 'T').

This is inspired by Satriani's work, meaning that I have slightly changed to make it more personal and meaningful to me. To do the above, simply play the 'e' string throughout and where directed, use the left finger to tap a fret position, let it play once, and then leave it for the next two strokes and move on to the next fret position. Try it yourself. Once done, we can then move on.

There is an alternate version to play this. Considering that you are comfortable with stretching your fingers a little, and are trying to create a different sound, you can use pull-offs instead. The result may hold the same notes, but the sound would be quite different. Both ways are fabulous and both ways get the job done, so feel free to experiment here as well.

Try and play the C Major seventh arpeggio shown below. Use your right hand to tap on the farthest note from your left hand (sometimes indicated with 'T2') and then use

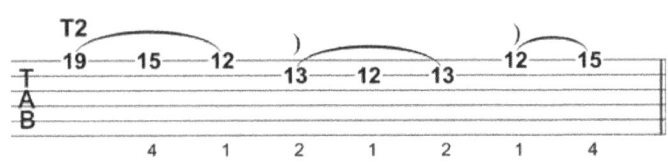

your left hand to pick out the remaining notes. For your convenience, you can also find the finger numbers to further help you play better.

Sounds nice, doesn't it? Timing matters a lot for tapping, so pay close attention to how accurately you can tap, to remain true to the tempo.

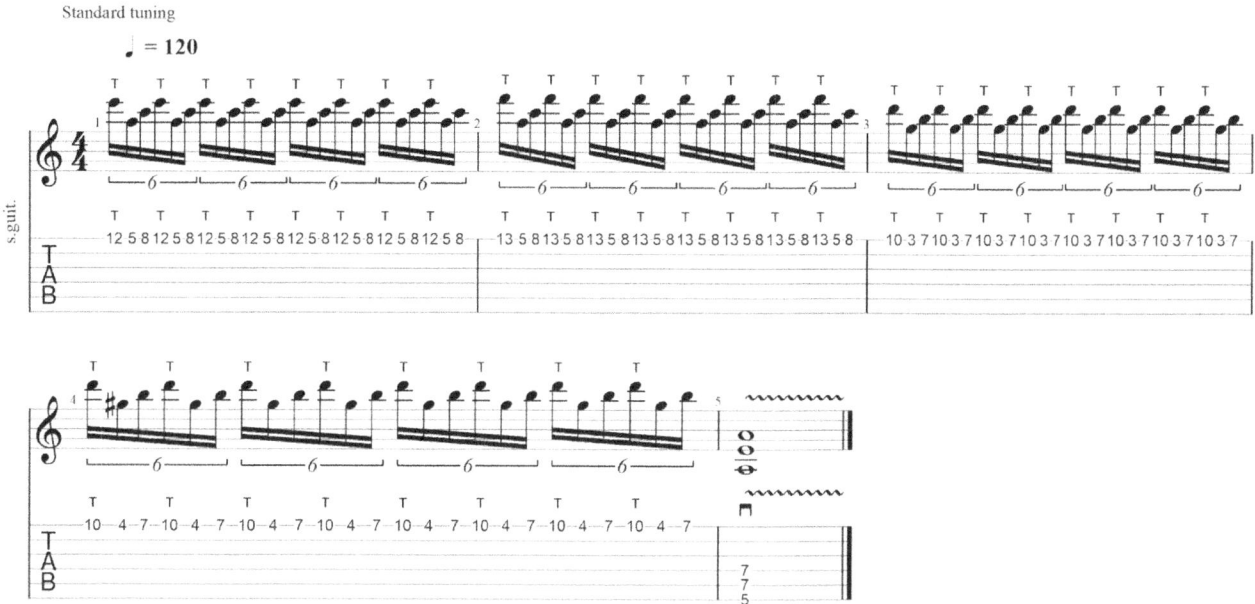

I can honestly say that this really takes me back to the days when Van Halen was ripping through the music world with his revolutionary techniques and music masterpieces. This is tough, but once you get the hang of it, you will never be looking to do anything else except use tapping.

Here is yet another in the style of **Van Halen**. This one uses A, Am, F, and Fadd9 chords.

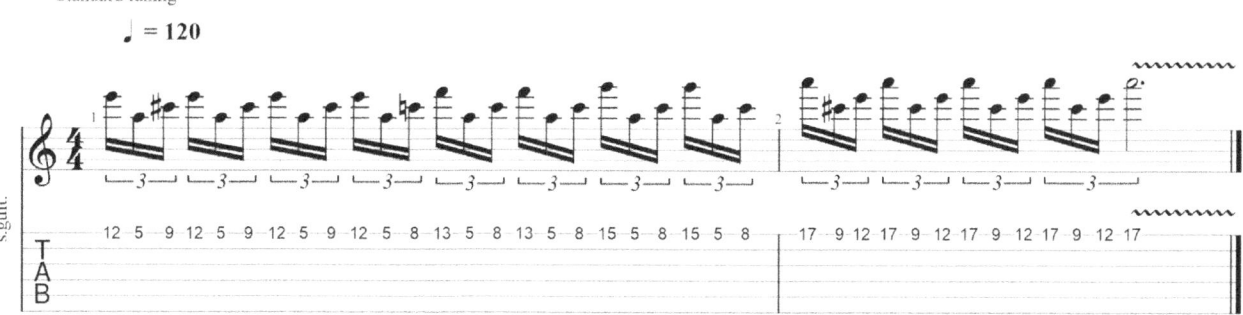

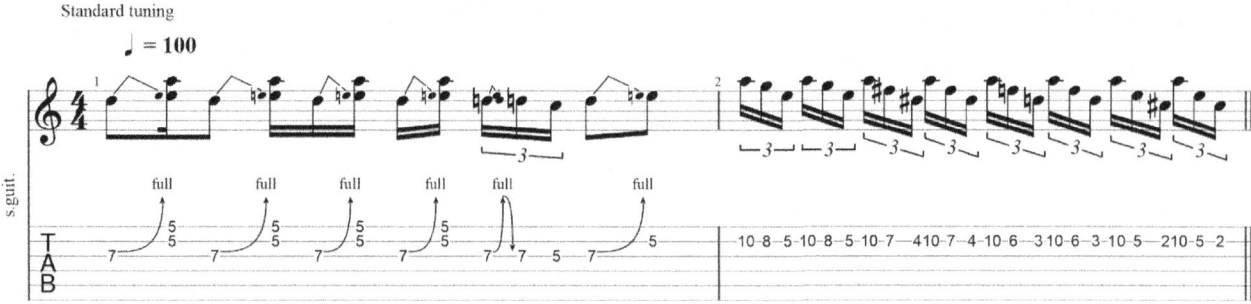

"Eddie Van Halen" by Clender is licensed under CC BY 2.0

I am sure you enjoyed the above two, which is why here is one more lick, played in the style of Eddie Van Halen. This time, we are using the A minor pentatonic scale to begin, ending at the A major pentatonic.

Here's a little challenge. Try and play the above by guessing which hand will remain over a single fret while the other hand moves. Yes! You keep your right hand on the 10th fret and then use the left hand to pick out other notes.

Well, now since you have a decent idea, let's look at some exquisite licks involving the use of tapping. Practice these and I promise you, you would be creating fans all over the place.

The Licks

Lick 1 — (Maj7 pattern)

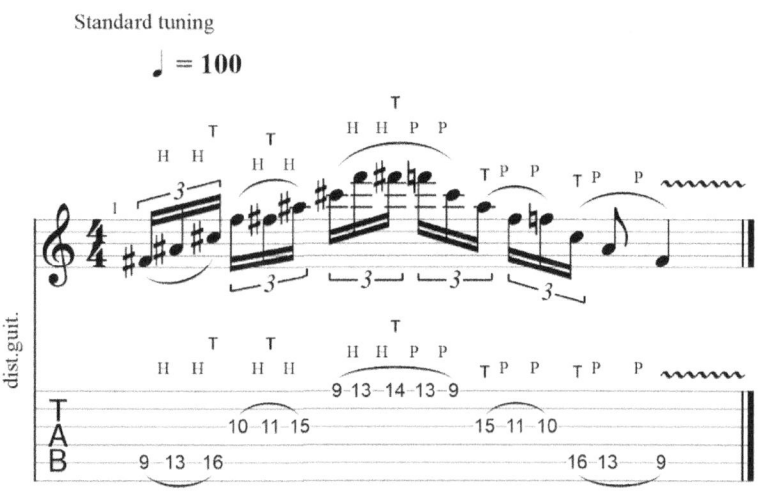

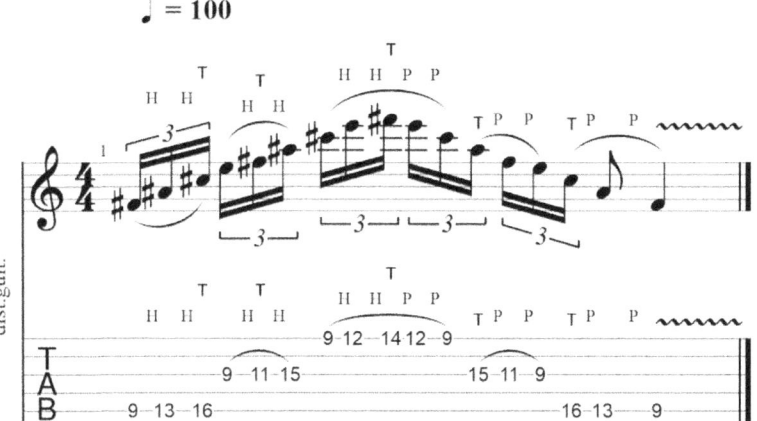

Lick 2 — (Dom7 Pattern)

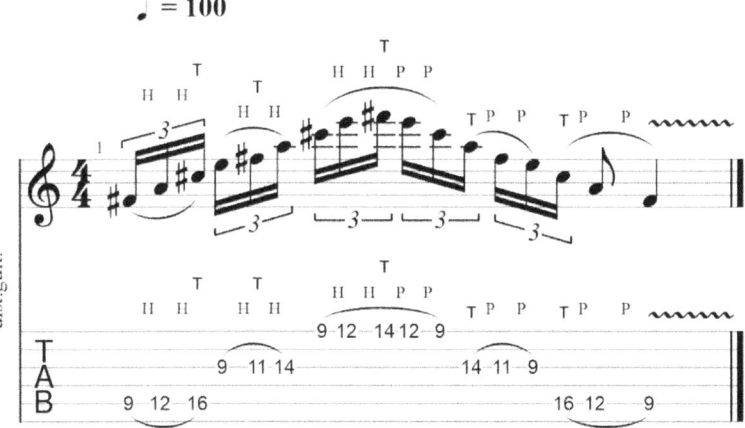

Lick 3 — (Min7 Pattern)

Lick 4 — (A combination of the above three)

Lick 5 — (A minor scale run)

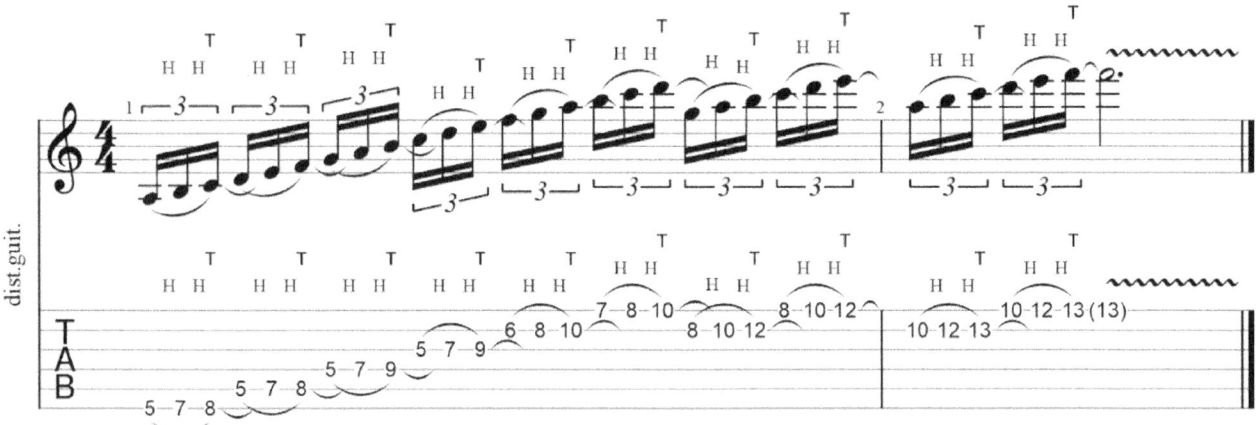

Lick 6 — (C Major Descending scale run)

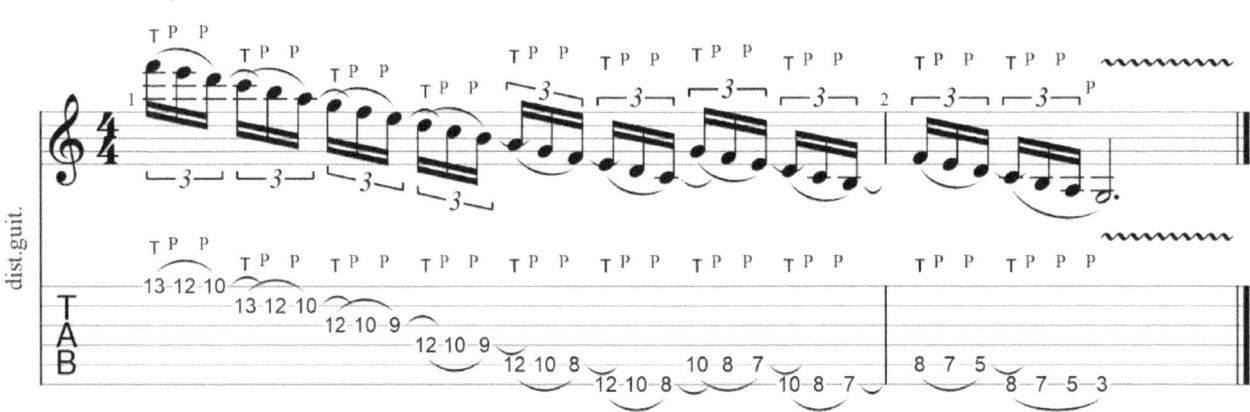

Lick 7 — (Variation of descending A minor pentatonic)

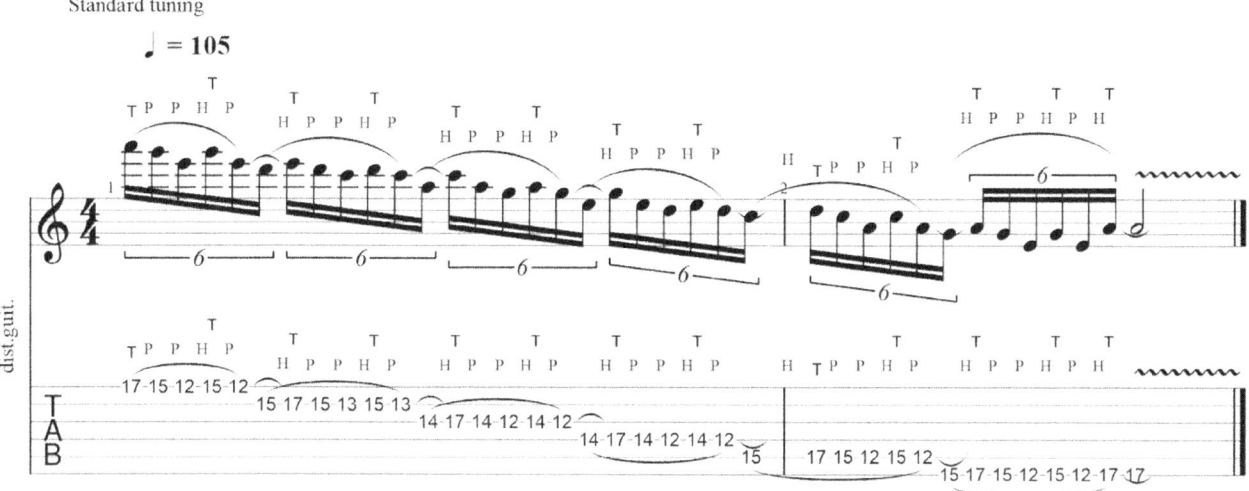

Lick 8 — (Neoclassical progression tapping lick — Em, D#dim7)

For the above, you can choose which note to tap on using your right hand, in case you are not able stretch your fingers wider.

Lick 9 — (A, Dm, A7, Dm)

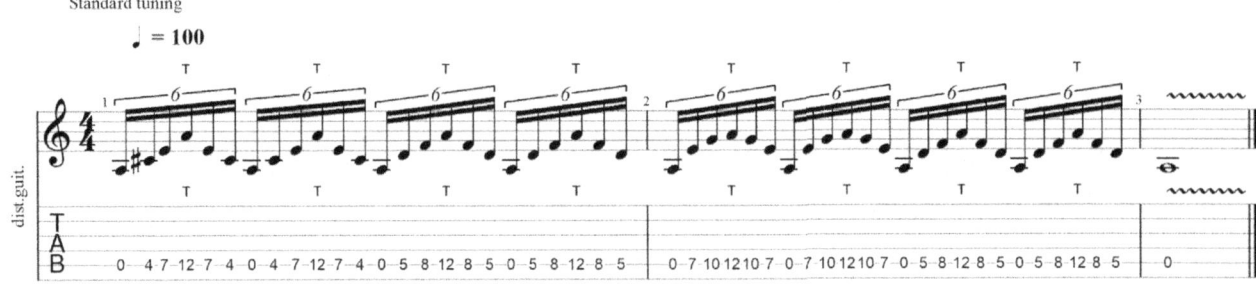

For this lick, play the open 'A' string with your tapping finger, but ensure that you do not touch the other strings. This is only for the first time as the rest would play automatically after a successful pull-off.

Lick 10 — (A minor on first string)

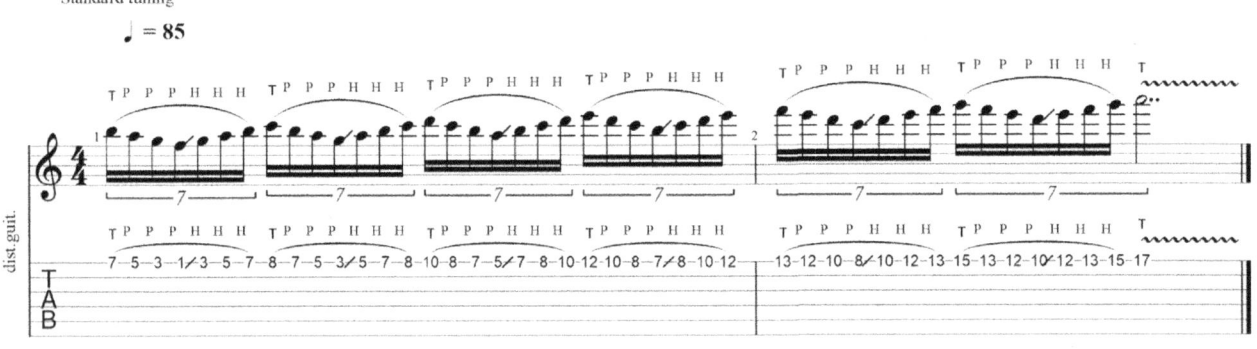

Lick 11 — (G minor pentatonic, string skipping exercise)

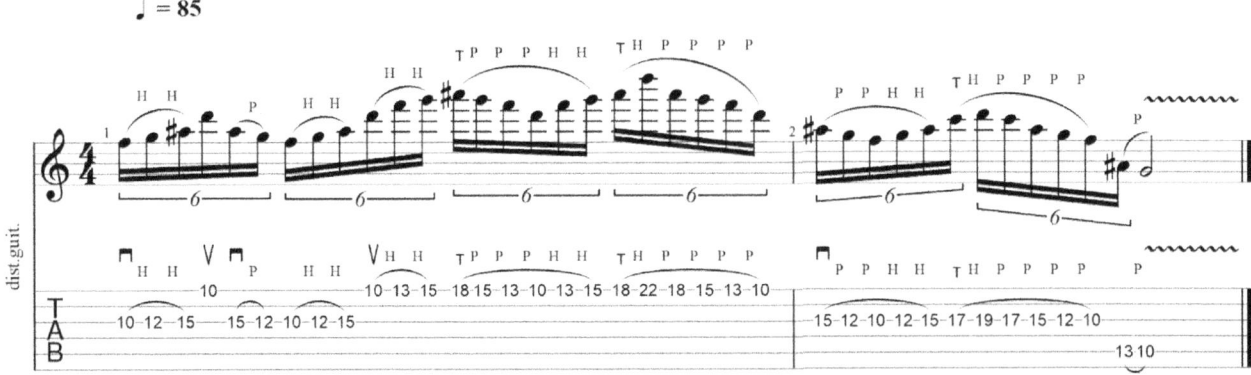

I am sure that your fingers are aching right about now by all that tapping. It is quite common for beginners to feel unusual pain sensations or numbness, or even develop calluses, and I am here to tell you that it is all part of the practice. We have all been there, and we managed to pull through using nothing more than our will to learn.

In the next chapter, we will look into harmonics. They may be slightly advanced, but once again, they are quite important to learn, especially if you are aiming to make this into a career.

CHAPTER 9:

Harmonics

Harmonics are what **Eric Johnson** would normally use in his songs or when he is on the stage. You may have actually played them yourself, however, you might have dismissed them as noise.

Every string has its natural harmonics. These are the purest forms of notes because the rest involve not only the sound of the note but the dampening effect of the string vibrating at the same time. However, there is a bit of technicality involved in playing harmonics, and while you can play harmonics on every string, you cannot go on to play harmonics on every fret position.

This chapter will look into this simple yet advanced technique to further up the ante and bring a new dimension to your playing. It is interesting, it is tricky, but in the end, it is something you would be thankful to learn.

Purity of Harmonics

First things first; harmonics can be played on all types of guitars, including acoustics, semis, and electric. To play a natural harmonic note, touch one of the following fret positions on any string gently. Do not press the fret as that would play out a note instead.

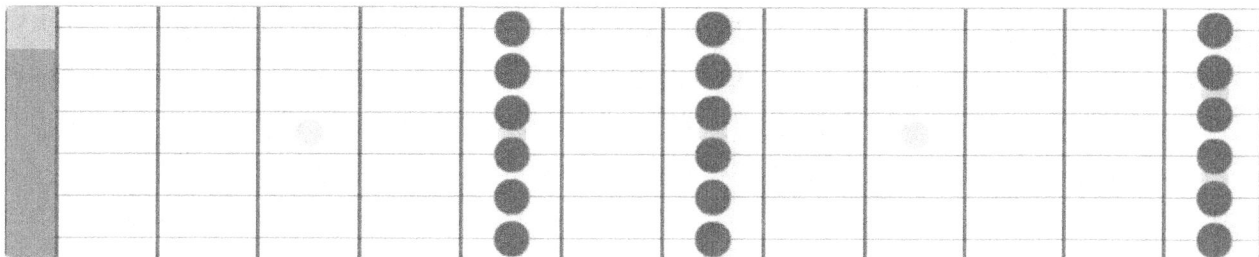

1. Fifth fret

2. Seventh fret

3. 12th Fret

See how crystal clear the sound is when you play a harmonic? You may have also noticed that they sound different from the actual note that lies on that specific position. This poses a bit of challenge for new guitarists. If you wish to use a harmonic on the fifth or seventh fret position, you must know which harmonic note lies on which of these frets and strings. Get that wrong and you may end up playing something that is completely irrelevant to the scale or key of the song.

> **SIDE NOTE:** *The natural harmonic on fifth and seventh fret position sounds an octave higher. For the 12th fret, the sound is exactly identical to the fretted note.*

Of course, it is natural that we will, at some point in time, want to include harmonics, but not the notes from these frets. Fortunately, there is a way to do that. While the above are natural harmonics, we can use something called touch harmonics. To do that, simply play and hold any note between first to 10th fret, and then use your right hand's finger (any) to touch the fret position that is an octave higher lightly. The result would create a touch harmonic.

Additionally, you can use something called pinch harmonic. This one is tricky to get, and requires a lot of trial and error before the actual technique is understood. To do this, play any note on any string, and then grip the pick between your thumb and the index finger so that it barely sticks out of your thumb. The idea is to pick the string so that it touches the little part of the pick, followed immediately by a light touch of your thumb. The result, when executed correctly, produces a harmonic for the note being played.

Finally, you have something called harp harmonics, and they make your guitar sound like a harp. This can be done by playing your right hand finger directly over the 12th fret (if using open string), touching the fret very lightly, and then using your thumb behind it to play the note. This will produce a harp-like sound. You can do the same for any note on any string as long as you place your right hand finger 12 frets higher and then play using the thumb.

When it comes to notation, or reading the harmonics, you will be able to spot them easily as they are denoted by a diamond-shaped note. In tablature, these are represented with a small dot next to the numbers. Furthermore, natural harmonics are represented with the "<fret number>" whereas the artificial ones are shown as "A.H" on top of tablature and the fret number followed by "<fret number + octave>."

The above is just an example to show how harmonics, whether artificial or otherwise, are written in music. Well, that's about it for the technique. It is now time to dive in and get ourselves a few decent licks.

Harmonically Beautiful Licks

Lick 1 — (Harp harmonic)

Lick 2 — (In style of Eric Johnson)

COLORADO SPRINGS, CO. USA MARCH 30: Guitarist Eric Johnson performs in concert March 30, 2012, at the Pikes Peak Center in Colorado Springs, CO. USA © TDCPhoto

Lick 3 — (in style of Eric Johnson)

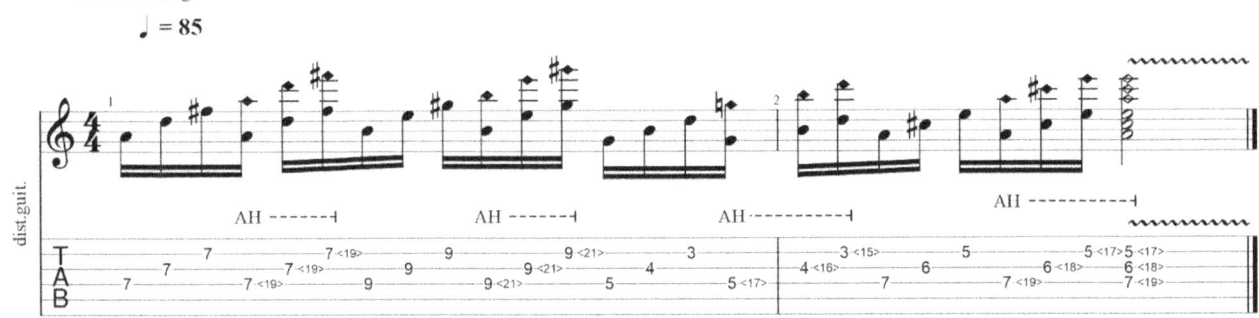

Lick 4 — (Natural Harmonic lick)

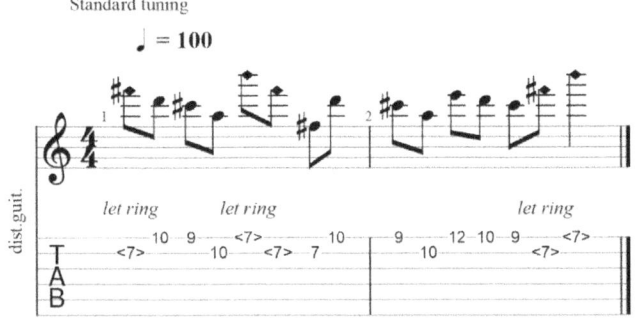

Harmonics are wonderful, especially if played right. Experiment with these and see how many you can start using in your songs and solos. If you use natural harmonics, and a clear effect, I would definitely recommend letting the note ring for a while.

Next stop, we will be looking at the iconic whammy bar and see how that can help us improve our playing.

CHAPTER 10:

Whammy Bar

Whammy bars are those pointy things sticking out of the bridge of the guitar, just near the volume and tone knobs. If you have followed **Steve Vai**, you would have seen him using that quite a lot to produce some intense and dramatic sounds.

Whammy bars are used by other artists too. These include the likes of **Jeff Beck** and **Scott Henderson.**

With that said, whammy bars come in different shapes and perform a variety of functions, and not all of them may be useful to us all. This chapter looks into how we can set it up, use it, the pros and cons, and finally the licks that we can use with whammy bars.

Understanding the Whammy Bar

Whammy bars are designed to create a string-bending like effect. However, we can only bend a string so much, and when you really need to take things up a notch, you use the whammy bar to bend it by a significant margin.

These are also used to create a tremolo effect, thus adding motion to the sound. It may sound a lot like a vibrato, but experienced guitarists will be able to spot the difference easily.

There are two types of guitars which offer the whammy bar or the tremolo. The first is the non-locking tremolo bridge guitar and the other is the locking tremolo bridge guitar. Both get the job done, and both allow for greater creativity to flow.

Now you might be thinking of getting a guitar with a tremolo bridge, there are some pros and cons you should go through before you make the purchase.

Pros

- Whammy bar phrasing
- Rhythmic riffs created using the bar
- Stretch or decompress strings to create effects like those of Satriani or Vai

Cons

- Strings will need constant tuning
- Difficult to use if you are using multiple tunings
- Constant adjustments of the whammy bar, to ensure you are not obstructed when playing regularly
- Risk of snapping strings

Choosing to go for a whammy bar or not is completely your call. I do not say that this piece of equipment is essentially necessary, but if you are looking to use it, I will certainly recommend buying yourself a guitar with floyd rose locking bridge. It keeps your guitar tuned longer than its counterpart, and it offers more flexibility.

Types of Whammy Bars

Remember I said that an experienced player would be able to identify if a whammy bar is used to create a vibrato effect? To solve that problem, someone back in the day came up with a few types of these bars. Some do one thing better than the other, and that is good news for us.

There are essentially four types of bars you can find for yourself.

1. Bigsby vibrato — Used to create vibrato effects

2. Fender synch tremolo — Used to create a tremolo effect

3. Locking tremolo

4. Floating bridge

All of these are great, but once again, each of them have some drawbacks or limitations, which we have discussed earlier. Using them, however, does create a massive room for exploring more creative ideas, as we will see in the next section.

Using these is fairly simple. Play a note or strum a chord, and push the bar down, release, pull up, and release. The downwards push would push the notes to go down the octave while the opposite will push the notes to go higher up. Repeated motion would create a wave-like feeling where the notes would sound as if they are moving (think vibrato on steroids).

Now, let's get to the fun part, shall we?

The Moving Licks

Lick 1 — (Minor Pentatonic — Using Tremolo effect)

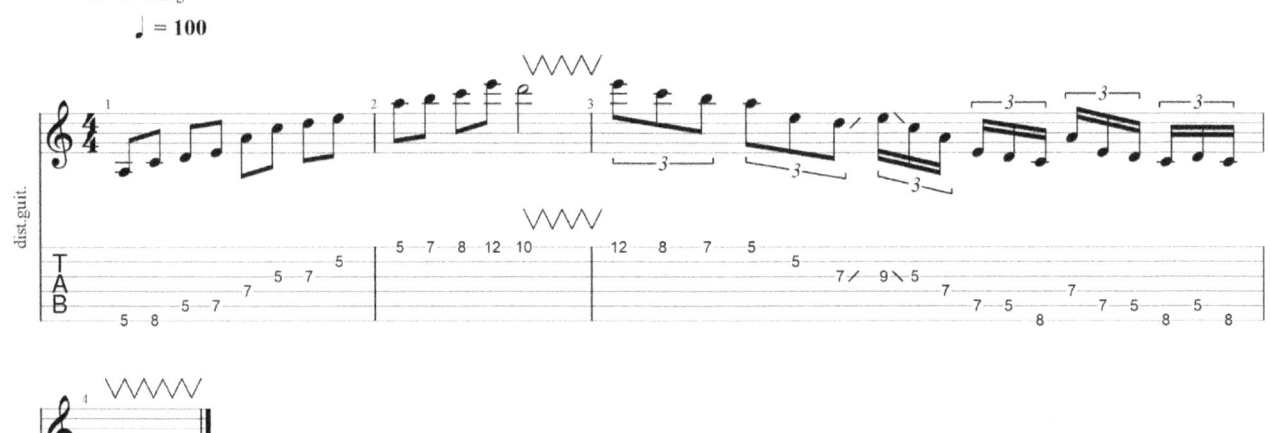

Lick 2 — (A minor pentatonic, B minor pentatonic, E minor pentatonic)

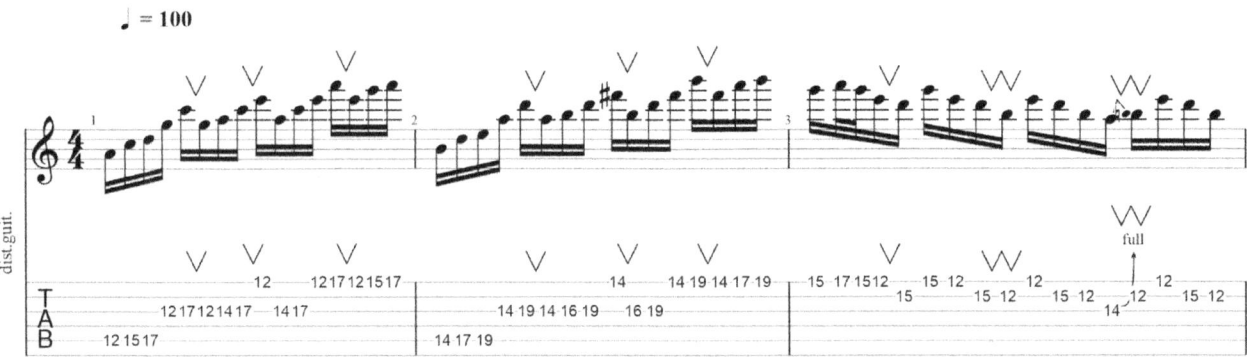

Lick 3 — (A Minor Pentatonic)

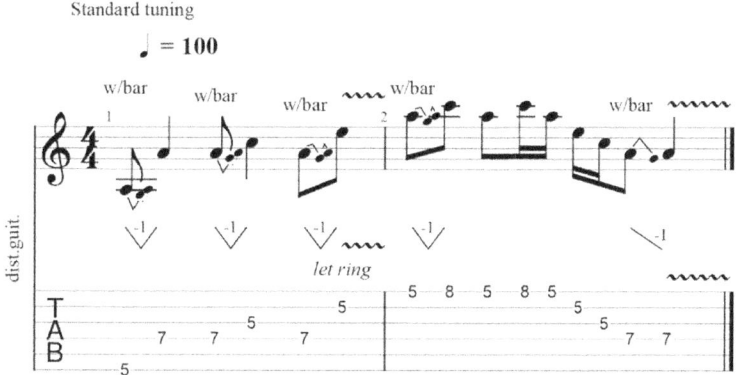

Lick 4 — (Gargling effect — tap the bar firmly after playing the note in place of your usual vibrato)

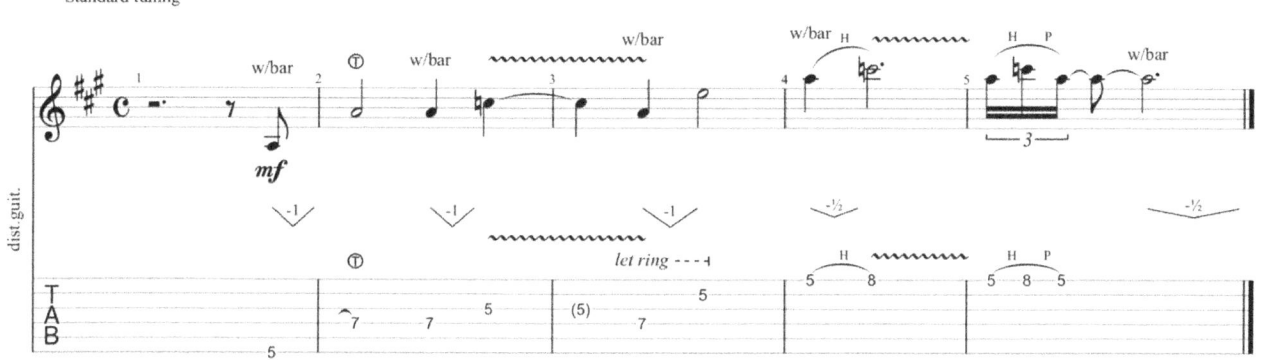

Lick 5 — (Slide effect)

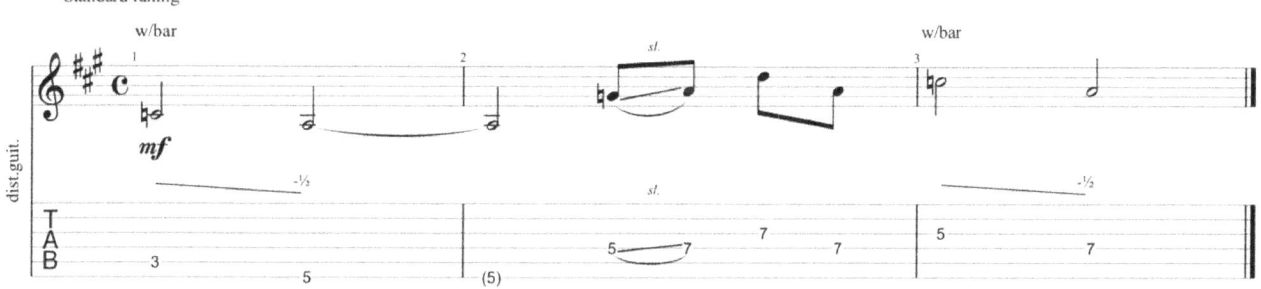

This is a continuation of the above, but it is where you can use the whammy bar to create a slow sliding effect.

Lick 6 — (Gargling effect + Slide in C Major)

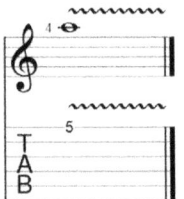

Lick 7 — (In style of Steve Vai)

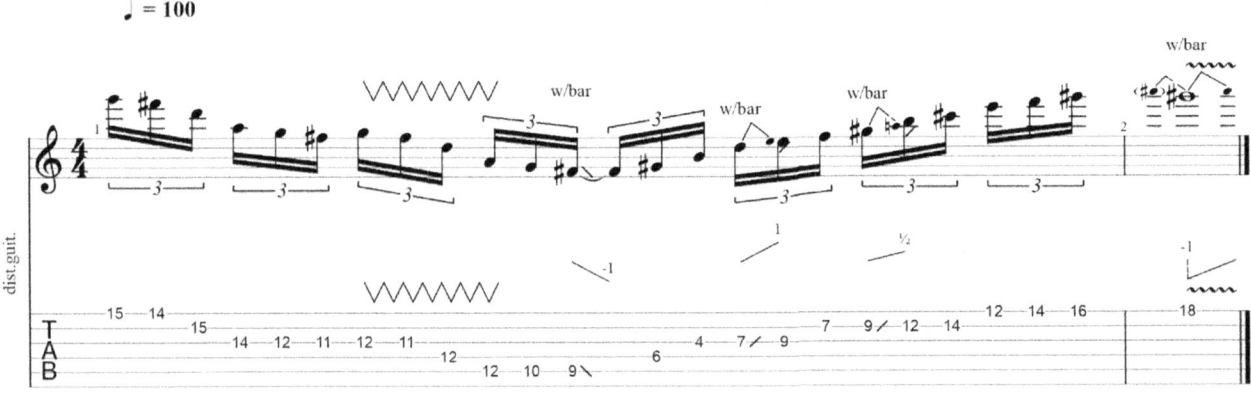

Lick 8 — (In style of Steve Vai — chromatic run)

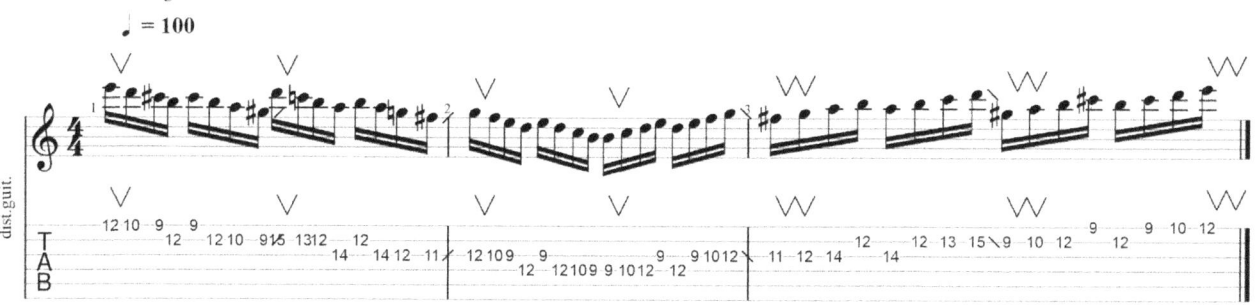

Lick 9 — (Dive bombing with Whammy bar)

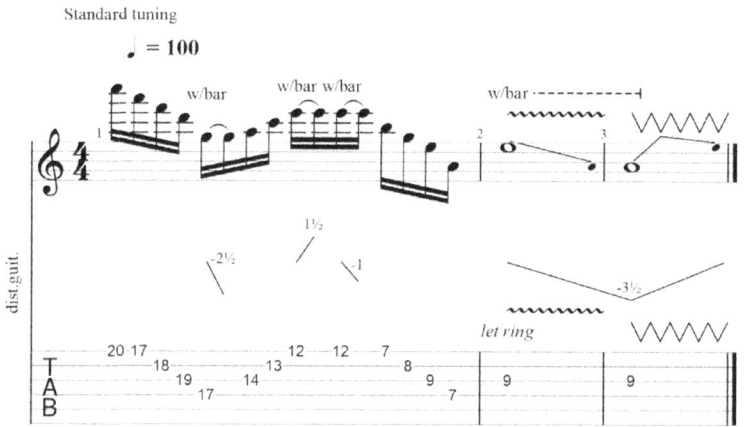

For the diving bomb effect, play the note and then push the bar down so that it changes the note by the number of half-steps shown. In the end, simply release the bar gradually to create a reverse dive bomb effect.

Lick 10 — (Pinch harmonics and dips)

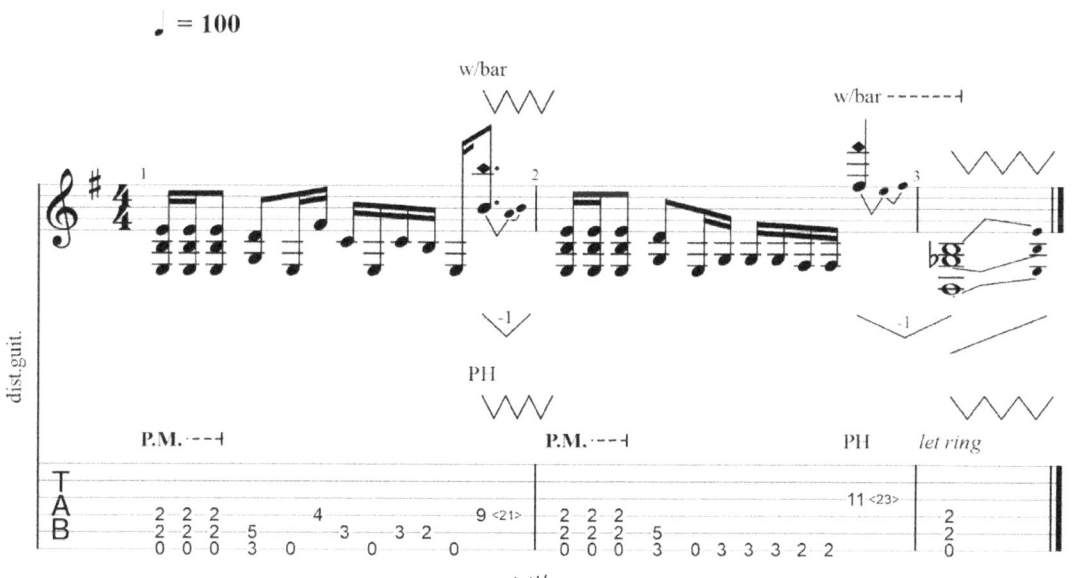

Lick 11 — (Pinch Harmonic — A5, G5)

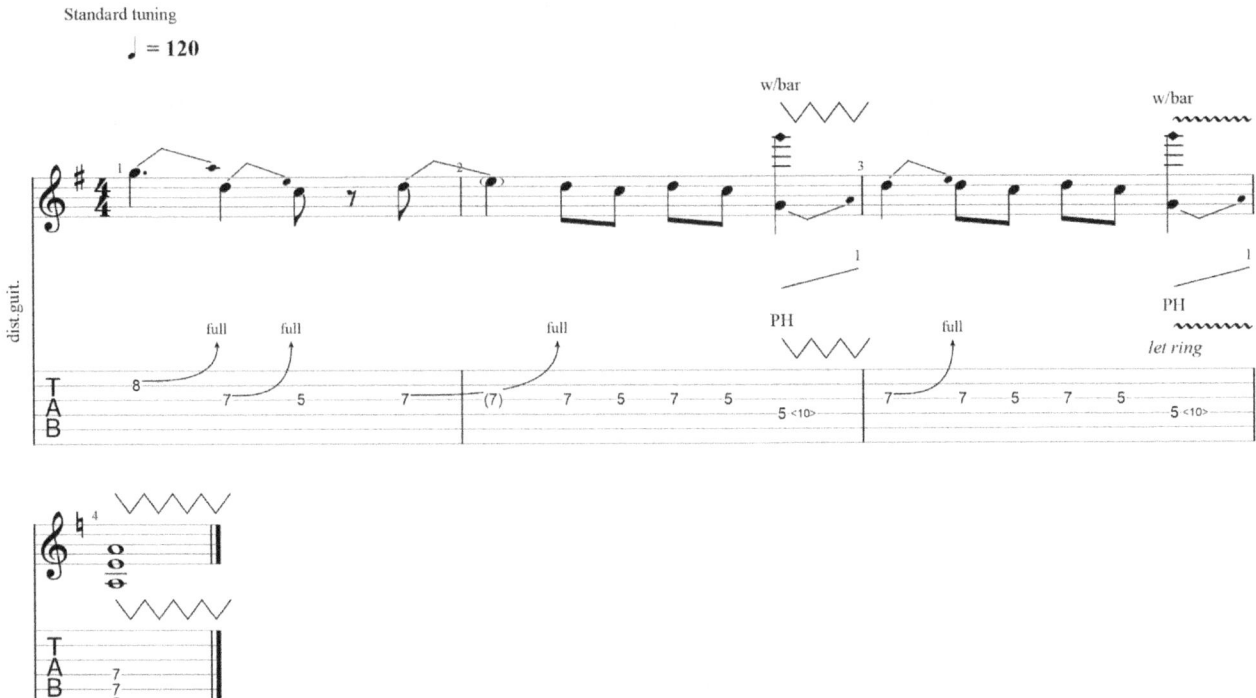

You have been doing extremely well so far, and I am sure you will soon be pulling off solos and riffs the likes of which no one around you expected you to do. However, I am not done yet. There is but one final part that we need to cover before I can say goodbye to you for now. The next chapter is where we will learn about octave playing, and it is pound for pound one of the finest techniques to learn.

CHAPTER 11:

Octave Playing

Octave playing is essentially playing a note along with another note that is perfectly 12 frets or an octave above the first note.

Guitarists around the world incorporate this simple exercise in playing a variety of licks, riffs, rhythms and even use these as great fillers. This chapter, therefore, is rather simple as there is not much technicality involved. However, this does not mean that you cannot use octave playing coupled with any of the techniques you learned previously. I encourage you to do so, and for inspiration, you can always listen to **Wes Montegomery**, who essentially is one of the finest when it comes to octave playing.

You can use this technique to either play the notes one after the other, or play them at the same instance. Both would produce melodic results, and will allow you to decide which one is better for your situation.

Getting the Basics

We know that an octave contains 12 notes. This means that if I was to play the note 'C' on any string, the next 'C' note I encounter as I travel upwards will have one octave value higher than the first one. The principle for this technique remains the same. The idea is to play a note and it's octave note either together or separately, just to create a more melodic experience.

Let us look at some basic licks first before moving on to slightly more advanced ones.

Lick 1 — (octaves played separately)

Lick 2 — (octaves played together)

Hopefully, you get the idea of how the octave playing works. Now, this seemingly simple technique is about to get a lot more challenging than just playing the G major with ease.

Octave licks

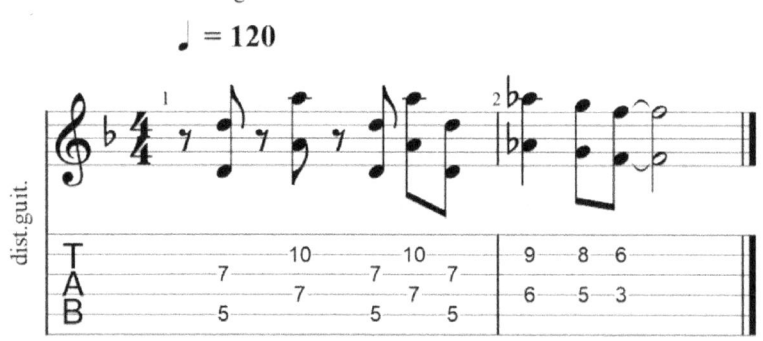

Lick 1 — (Dm7)

Lick 2 — (Dm7)

Lick 3 — (Dm7(b5), G7 (alt), Cm7)

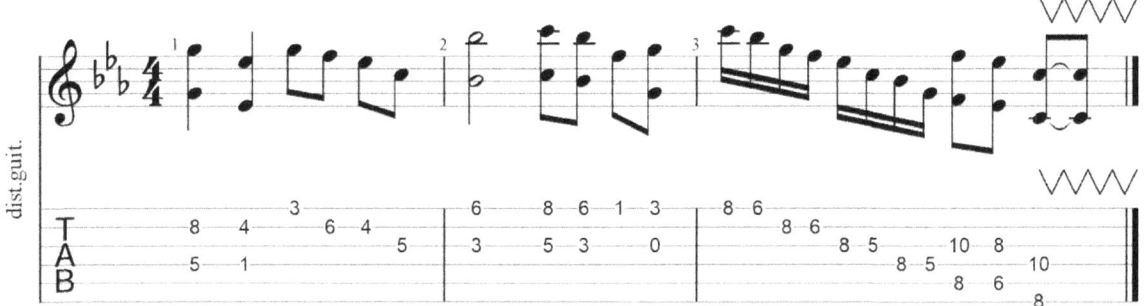

Lick 4 — (In style of Wes, with Gm7, Em7(b5) and A7(alt))

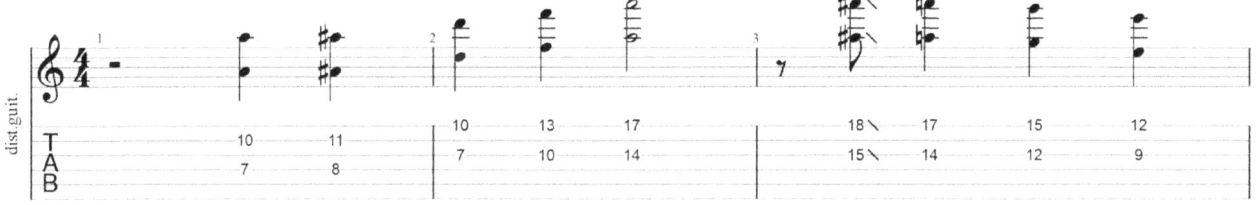

Lick 5 — (Wes style, Fmaj7, Em7(b5), A7(alt), Dm7)

Lick 6 — (In style of George Benson, Dm9, Dm, Am9, Dm7)

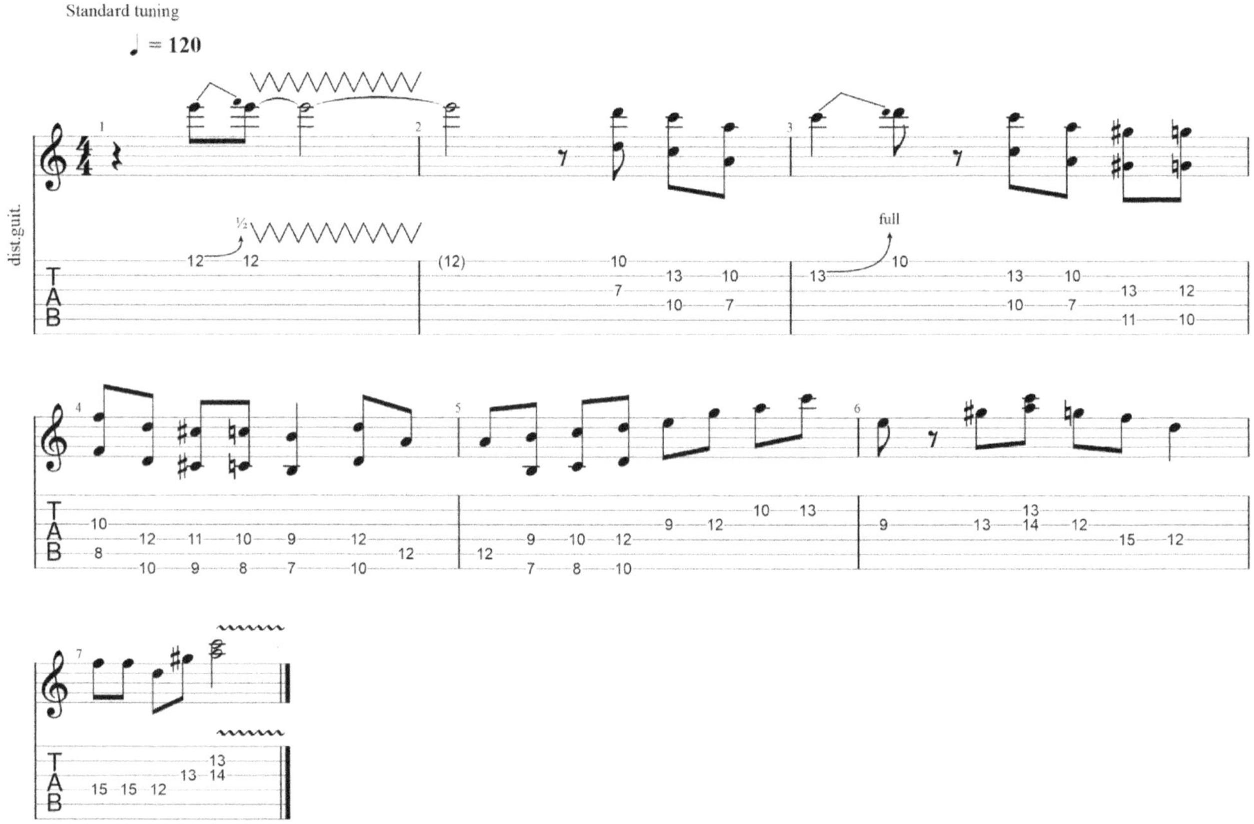

And there you have it. Licks which sound nice and are equally fun to play.

12-14 July 2019. North Sea Jazz Festival, Ahoy Rotterdam, The Netherlands. Concert of George Benson
@ benhoudijk

While our journey may have come to an end, it is only a beginning for you. Yes, there is a lot that needs to be learned, and most of it will come through experience. While you can find as many books online as you desire, the true learning is done by what you experience, play, realize and create.

With that said, I leave you with nothing but best wishes, and hope that this book has served you with knowledge and has instilled a sense of confidence that you have everything you need to get out there and start impressing some serious people.

I certainly do hope that you will continue to practice all that you have learned, and that you will also modify some of these to further personalize these licks. Rules are meant to be broken, and it is only by breaking these musical rules (not the actual ones) that you can learn how to further push your creativity. Never lose hope, and always stick to the basics when everything seems intimidating. The rest will come to you, I promise you that.

Farewell!

Pssssstttt....

What are you doing here? Are you lost?

Do people even look at the last pages of a book?

Jokes aside, I hope you enjoyed this book. I certainly loved the process of writing it — a short and to the point book!

I am not the kind of person who writes long goodbyes thanking every celestial body. So here is Guitar Head signing off!

Until next time then? I'll see you in my next book.

THE END